I0055914

THE

MILLIONAIRE
MONEY MOVES
SUPPLEMENTAL
INVESTMENT
GUIDE

THE

MILLIONAIRE MONEY MOVES

SUPPLEMENTAL INVESTMENT GUIDE

CEDRIC NASH

Founder of the Black Wealth Summit

HOUNDSTOOTH
PRESS

The Millionaire Money Moves Supplemental Investment Guide

ISBN 978-1-5445-3653-8 *Hardcover*
    978-1-5445-3654-5 *Paperback*
    978-1-5445-3655-2 *Ebook*

CONTENTS

SECURITIES INVESTING

Stocks, Bonds, and Commodities

WELCOME BACK! LET'S TAKE THAT NEWFOUND FIRE IN YOUR belly and put it in service of building some concrete wealth. The following four subchapters focus on leveraging the lessons you've learned and building a portfolio of investments that aligns with your risk tolerance, all the while keeping your money working for you. No matter which investment area or areas you go into, your purpose will be to constantly build up capital to either start and run your own business or to expand and amplify your investment portfolio. So, let's begin with investing in securities.

Rather than make recommendations on which securities to buy and when to buy them, I'm going to focus on the process of investing to achieve Destination Millionaire. I'll leave that other discussion for your financial adviser or investment team, or to the authors of the thousands of books that already exist on the subject. However, because investing in securities is so critical to your wealth journey, it's essential that we at least take a broad look at how to use the stock market to build wealth. Some of the terms I'll be discussing may at first sound like Latin or ancient Greek to you, but with effort, practice, and consistency over time, you will begin to recognize and understand them as easily as you do a Brooklyn accent or a Southern lilt. The same is true of market concepts, like the idea that you can make money on the way up, or you can make money on the way down. In other words, whether the market wins or loses doesn't dictate whether you win or lose. What matters is when you buy or sell your assets. A great example of why that matters was the calamitous drop in the stock market when the COVID-19 pandemic first hit in March 2020, which was followed by the roaring return of the market to previous all-time highs. The folks who bought when the market collapsed and sold or held on to their investments when it recovered turned a handsome profit even at the so-called worst of times.

WHAT IS SECURITIES INVESTING?

Simply put, securities investing means buying shares of stock, bonds, or commodities, such as oil, corn, wheat, and so forth. It allows you to grow your capital rapidly, so you can make other types of capital-intensive investments later and dramatically grow your wealth. Millionaires know where their bread is baked, and so should you. Since its inception in the 1920s, the stock market has produced an annual return—over time—about 10 percent, which is why it is no accident that approximately 84 percent of stocks in the US are owned by the wealthiest 10 percent.[1]

---

[1] Robert Gebeloff, "Who Owns Stock? Explaining the Rise in Inequity During the Pandemic," *The New York Times*, January 26, 2021, www.nytimes.com/2021/01/26/upshot/stocks-pandemic-inequality.html.

The stock market is an incredible tool for investors, both new and seasoned. You can get started in it with just a little capital. Your investments are "liquid," meaning you can turn them back into cash, within hours, if necessary. The odds favor your success if you use the tool properly and think of securities as long-term investments. You can even use a very small percentage of your capital—money you can afford to part with—for riskier plays in the market.

Yet equally important as what securities investments you make is why you make them in the first place. Without clear goals about why you're investing in the stock market, you stand a good chance of wasting a lot of time and your money going nowhere. Three of the most common reasons to invest in securities are to get rich by "hitting the jackpot," to achieve steady growth for your capital over time, or to generate income. This book is about steady growth over time and income generation. I realize that some of you may be looking to hit the jackpot; if so, you will not only need a sizable amount of capital, but you'll also have to time the market by trading (buying and selling) often. A more conservative approach is to steadily grow the value of your account with a diversified portfolio of securities. The most conservative of all three goals is to generate income by investing in stable, blue-chip companies that pay dividends, even though they offer little relative valuation and slow growth in their stock price. The perspective I believe most emerging millionaires should adopt is that there is only one surefire way to make money in securities, and that way is "slowly." Carefully accumulating and holding onto shares of well-managed, profitable companies over time can ensure that you eventually arrive at Destination Millionaire safely.

My personal securities investment goal is to achieve steady growth of my capital over time; to in essence put my money to work safely while avoiding unnecessary risks of capital loss before I reach retirement age. At that point, I plan to focus on preserving my capital while generating income from my investment portfolio. I am what the market calls a "retail" investor, and I don't plan to become a trader anytime soon (in other words, never). That suits me and my financial goals just fine. Your approach to securities investing should also be based on who you are and what suits you, not on some character you saw on the show *Billions*. The most reliable decision is to become a smart, evolving retail investor and leave the high-risk, capital-intensive "trading" to the others.

Before we go further in discussing investing in securities, let's go over some key terms and definitions that will help you better understand securities investing.

KEY TERMS AND DEFINITIONS YOU'LL NEED TO START INVESTING IN SECURITIES

My goal for now is to make you familiar with and confident enough in securities investing to get started right away and to put you on the path to continuous learning. Even someone like Russell L. Goings, the first Black brokerage manager at a NY Stock Exchange firm, continues to read and learn about investing and the companies he invests in. Your immediate goal is to become an investor with a solid working knowledge of securities investment, rather than a trader who buys and sells securities based on years or decades of expertise. Here is a tiny subset of the terms you'll need to understand to get started investing in securities.

STOCKS OR EQUITIES

A stock, or equity, is a fractional ownership piece in a company. If I said you could buy half my company and my company had a total of one hundred shares, half the company would amount to fifty shares. The difference with publicly traded companies is that they are made up of millions of shares which are bought and sold on stock exchanges. The reason they're called shares is that you share in the company's assets and profits, proportionally, when you own their stock. The more stock you own, the greater your percentage of any eventual profits or dividends. In addition to purchasing individual stocks, you can purchase groups of stocks, known as funds.

Index Funds

An index fund is a "basket" of securities (stocks and bonds) that you can invest in as a pool of investments rather than having to buy each individual stock. Probably the best-known index fund is the S&P (Standard & Poor's) 500, which tracks the performance of five hundred large cap (capitalization) stocks traded on the American stock exchanges. An index fund is a great way to passively invest in the overall performance of the stock market or a particular sector of the market, instead of having to pick and choose winners and losers one at a time. Naturally, the returns on index funds are smaller because the risk is smaller.

Index funds have become wildly popular over the past several years. They offer lower fees than mutual funds because they are self-managed, meaning there is no fund manager to pay for choosing the stocks, nor for trading them on a regular basis.

Exchange Traded Funds (ETFs)

An exchange traded fund, or ETF, is a type of security that follows the performance of an index, commodity, sector, or another asset. Rather than buying a single stock, an ETF allows individuals to invest in the performance of a group of similar stocks or assets. Some of the best-known ETFs are the S&P 500 Index or the Dow Jones Industrials (DJI). Like individual stocks, ETFs are required to be easily bought and sold on an exchange. Many ETFs are self-managed, resulting in lower fees and better tax efficiency.

Mutual Funds

Mutual funds are "baskets" of securities shared in a pooled investment portfolio among many investors. They can either be actively managed by a team of money managers, passively managed according to rules-based investment criteria, or pegged to securities in an index. Mutual funds invest in a wide variety of stocks selected by the fund manager. The fees are higher because there is a manager, and if the investments underperform, those fees can erode your account balance in a hurry. Mutual funds exploded in popularity in the 1980s and '90s, and as a result, the same model was adopted to invest in a wide variety of securities spanning not only the stock and bond markets but real estate and commodities as well. However, with the wide variety of investment options within mutual funds comes a wide variety of fees and expenses that investors should be aware of.

BONDS

A bond, also known as a "fixed instrument," is a loan that an investor makes to a borrower. US Treasury bonds, for example, are loans made by investors to the US government in exchange for a promise of repayment and interest. Bonds are used by governments, companies, municipalities, and states to finance projects and operations, such as expansion, infrastructure, and so forth. As with any loan, a bond comes with detailed information as to when the loan is payable, what the interest rate is, and whether that interest rate is fixed or variable.

STOCK TRADER

A stock trader, also known as a broker, is a professional purchaser and seller of stocks and bonds. Increasingly, individual investors are bypassing brokers and making online trades themselves, through platforms like Robinhood and Vanguard. While that's undoubtedly a positive trend, especially since those platforms don't charge fees to trade, those individuals are people who trade stocks, not stock traders—the same way a person singing in the shower is not a professional singer. Stockbrokers have years of experience and exposure to information that is generally out of reach to people like us. That doesn't necessarily make them smarter or better at choosing stocks, though it does make them better informed.

PORTFOLIO

A portfolio is like a virtual wallet which contains all your securities investments: stocks, bonds, cash equivalents including closed-end funds, ETFs, and cash.

DIVIDENDS

Remember how we said that buying stock means owning shares in a company and its profits? Dividends are payments of some of those profits, also known as "earnings," as determined by the company's board of directors. Not all companies pay dividends; those that do, pay their dividends proportional to your level of stock ownership, either as cash or as additional stock. The more stock you own in a company, the higher the dividend you'll receive. Since you're investing in actual companies when you purchase shares in them, whenever those companies do well, they not only become more valuable in terms of share price, but they also make profits that they can either reinvest in the business or pay out as dividends to investors like you. With a little research, as simple as googling, "Which companies pay dividends to investors?" you can easily figure it out and invest in them accordingly. What I like best about dividends is that they make me feel like, while I'm waiting for my stocks to go up in price, there's a guy walking around handing out hundred-dollar bills as a reward for my patience. That sounds like a pretty sweet deal to me. As you transition to retirement and have built up your Freedom Fund, dividend stocks are a popular way to generate income in retirement. The larger the Freedom Fund, the larger your investment retirement income will be.

DIVERSIFICATION

One of the most important risk management strategies we've discussed is the idea that your risk as an investor needs to be spread out. Your portfolio should become a rainbow of asset types (stocks, bonds, ETFs, and other securities), and those securities themselves should vary in their degree of risk and yield length. This type of strategic diversification is the difference between fighting with a navy instead of one or two big battleships. It's much harder to sink a navy. Some studies have shown that a diversified portfolio, meaning twenty-five to thirty stocks, is an optimum level in terms of cost efficiency and risk reduction. More than that doesn't necessarily generate higher efficiency, though there's certainly nothing wrong with further diversifying your portfolio. What must be avoided at all costs is too little diversification.

STOCK SPLITS

Occasionally a company's board of directors will decide to increase the number of shares available to current shareholders by splitting the stock. They might double the number in a two-for-one split, quadruple the number in a four-one split, and so forth. For you as an investor, this would only mean that the number of shares you already own would increase by a factor of two or four, but the price of each share would be halved or quartered. For instance, one share of Coca-Cola selling for $100 would become two shares of Coca-Cola selling for $50 each. Now that the overall price is lower, the stock may be more in reach of smaller investors. Some companies, such as Berkshire Hathaway, choose to never split their stocks, resulting in an astronomical price per share over time.

PROSPECTUS

When a company offers its shares for sale to the public, it's required to file a formal document called a "prospectus," which provides details about the investment offering and the company. A prospectus is roughly analogous to a one-sheet in real estate, a deeper look into the home (or in this case, the company) you're interested in buying.

BEAR AND BULL MARKETS

Markets are cyclical in nature. A bear market describes a market experiencing prolonged price declines of 20 percent or more. A bull market is the opposite: extended price increases that can last for months and often years. If an investor says they're "bullish" about a company, it means they're expecting the company's stock price to rise. "Bearish" means their outlook is pessimistic.

OPTIONS (PUTS AND CALLS)

Options are financial derivatives that give buyers the right, but not the obligation, to buy or sell an underlying asset at an agreed-upon price and date. Options to buy and sell are a way for investors to minimize risk and reduce the capital they need to have available in their stock portfolio. Rather than buy an asset outright, investors purchase a low-priced option to buy the asset later, at a set price, known as a "call." If the asset fails to reach the set price in time, the option expires, and the investor loses the small bit of money they paid for the call option. If instead the asset reaches or exceeds that price within the set time, the investor can then buy it outright at the agreed-upon price. If the price is higher than had been agreed to, the investor keeps the profit. A "put" is the opposite of a call; it's an option to sell a stock at a set price and time. In that case, the lower the share price goes, the better it is for the option holder. If you owned a put option to sell XYZ stock at $50 per share by next Friday and the price went down to $25 per share by then, you could exercise your option, sell the stock for $50 per share, and keep the $25-per-share profit. Puts and calls allow investors to choose whether they think a stock is going up or down in price and make money in either direction. Whether an investor buys a call or a put, they are under no obligation to exercise the option (meaning buy or sell the asset) if they choose not to.

MARGIN TRADING

Margin trading is using borrowed money to buy stock based on the value of your account or holdings that serve as collateral. The same way you can buy a home with a down payment and get a bank to finance the rest, if you have sufficient collateral, you can buy a stock for a percentage of its full price and get a brokerage house to finance the rest. The amount you borrow is called the "margin." Due to the volatile nature of stock markets, the margin loan to value or "margin requirement" is typically 50 percent on listed company stocks. This means you can buy, for example, $50,000 worth of XYZ stock (one thousand shares at $50 per share) with only

$25,000 down. However, if the share price dips below $50 per share, then you must absorb that loss by putting additional funds into your margin account so that the brokerage house doesn't lose money on their part of the investment. That's the inherent risk of margin trading. If the share price goes up, on the other hand, all the profits belong to you.

THE PROS AND CONS OF SECURITIES INVESTING

There are a host of solid reasons to invest in securities. You can quickly turn a little bit of money into a lot or else do so over time. Securities investment doesn't require a great deal of money to get started. Profits can be reinvested to generate even more money through compounding. Securities can be bought and sold with tremendous ease. You can leverage your account balance to borrow money and buy more stocks. And finally, many stocks generate income through the dividends they pay.

As with any investment strategy, securities investment also has some downsides. Stock selection can be extremely challenging and may require a good deal of reading and research. Prices can fluctuate significantly, including crashing or skyrocketing, without a moment's notice. Stock prices can even go as low as zero, which would mean losing your entire investment in them, and thus, your temperament, as well as your long-term strategy, play a critical role in how you approach securities investment.

MANAGING RISK IN SECURITIES INVESTMENT

Since the stock market is by its nature unpredictable, every investor needs strategies to protect themself if the market goes haywire or to put them in a position to ride the wave of prosperity whenever the big one comes in. The two best hedges, as they are known in the investment world, are diversification and Dollar Cost Averaging.

Through diversification, you can limit your losses and reduce the fluctuations of investment returns, without sacrificing too much potential gain, by selecting the right group of investments. It doesn't make sense to keep all your eggs in one basket. A correctly diversified asset allocation will have a major impact on whether you will meet your financial goals or not. At the same time, if you don't include enough risk in your portfolio, your investments may not earn a large enough return to meet your goal. For example, if you are saving for a long-term goal, such as retirement or college, most financial experts agree that you will likely need to include at least some stock or stock mutual funds in your portfolio. On the other hand, if you include too much risk in your portfolio, the money for your goal may not be there when you need it. For instance, a portfolio weighted too heavily in stocks or equity mutual funds, would be inappropriate for a time-sensitive, short-term goal, such as retiring in the next five years.

If you're not yet sure how to diversify, you can take the guesswork out of it by investing in index funds, exchange-traded funds, or mutual funds. Major brokerage firms, such as Schwab and Fidelity, provide basic advice that can help you get started and achieve adequate portfolio diversification. What matters is that your portfolio is diversified between asset categories as well as within asset categories. For example, you might invest in a tech-focused ETF as well as some individual stocks, but you want those individual stocks to encompass a wide range rather than putting all your money in only one or two stocks. You may want to invest in riskier "growth" stocks that are new to the stock exchanges. If so, you can simultaneously invest in less-volatile bonds or commodities to provide some balance to that risk. As in military combat, the more you spread out your assets, the less vulnerable they are to a concentrated attack, such as—in market terms—a downturn in an individual share price or sector of the market.

Dollar Cost Averaging, or DCA, is the most reliable method for establishing and maintaining consistency. It does so by preventing you from purchasing your entire portfolio at the height of the market and presenting opportunities to buy shares at lower points of the market. It's a dependable risk mitigation strategy that shields investors from the whims of the marketplace. DCA works like this: Suppose you think a blue-chip stock like Coca-Cola is a worthwhile investment over the long term (which historically, it is). Let's say the price of shares in Coca-Cola has been going up the past few months due to a new soft drink product in their line of beverages. That's good news for existing Coke shareholders but bad news for you if you want to buy in. You don't want to pay a premium price now for Coke stock, do you? Of course not. You want to buy Coca-Cola when the share price is down, not up. But when is that going to happen? No one can say.

Dollar Cost Averaging looks at this situation differently. In a DCA strategy, you—the investor—decide to buy four shares of Coca-Cola every month, regardless of the price, for three years or longer. Sometimes you'll get it at a more favorable price, say, whenever a rival like Pepsi manages to capture greater market share in the beverage space or comes out with their own new soft drink. Other times, you'll pay a higher price because Coke's stock is going up exactly as you'd hoped it would. But by being strategic and purchasing in this way, you reduce your exposure to the cyclical nature of the market—the very cycles that had you trying to guess when the share price would go down, so you could buy in—and you've successfully purchased an appreciating asset over the long term. The price you paid on average is somewhere lower than the highest price and somewhere higher than the lowest stock price. It's an average price per share as opposed to a high price per share, if you had purchased all your shares at the height of the market.

Here is a real-world example of DCA in action. Say you decided every month to buy $500 of an individual stock, such as Apple. Let's assume Apple is currently trading at $145.60 a share. Therefore, you'd be able to buy 3.43 shares ($500 $145.60 = 3.43) of Apple stock this month. If next month, the shares of Apple stock dropped to $100 per share, you would be able to buy 5 shares for $500 ($500 100 = 5). The average share price over those two months of $122.80 (($145.60 + $1002 = $122.80) over the two months is lower than the share price you paid at the time of your most expensive purchase ($145.60/share), but higher than the price you paid at the time of your least expensive purchase ($100/share). By using DCA to purchase Apple stock at a rate of $500 per month over the past ten years (adjusted for stock splits and after an initial investment of $500), the Apple portion of your portfolio would look like this:

Dollar Cost Averaging Apple Stock
From July 1, 2011 to April 31, 2018

Investment Activity

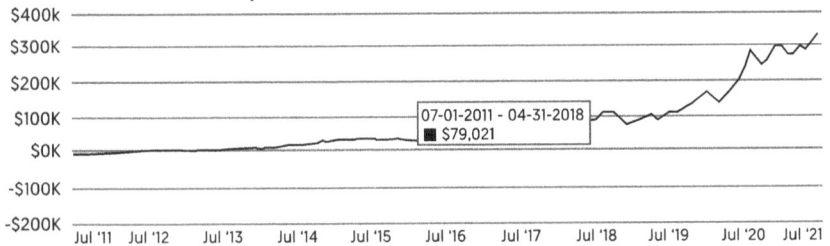

- Portfolio A

Performance

Initial investment	$500.00	Average annualized return	32.01%
Net amount invested	$60,500.00	Cumulative return	1,511.08%
Final market value	$330,387.77		

Your total investment, in that case, would amount to $60,500 and the value of that investment after ten years would be $330,387.77. Your average annualized return would be 32.01 percent with a cumulative return of 1,511.08 percent.

What I especially like about this strategy is how it dovetails perfectly with the type of steadfast courage I want you to bring to bear on your financial life. If you keep putting one foot in front of another, you will get to the glorious end you seek no matter how often market conditions change. Leave the sprinting for the hares at Goldman Sachs and Morgan Stanley. Consistency and long-term Dollar Cost Averaging is for the rest of us tortoises. Millionaire tortoises, that is.

Of course, your trip to Destination Millionaire isn't only about minimizing risk; it's also about maximizing profits. So, for now, I want you to get started at a level you feel comfortable with, and then we'll move on to how to make your investments grow exponentially over time.

UNIVERSAL STRATEGIES FOR SUCCESSFUL SECURITIES INVESTING

After years of dabbling in the stock market starting in 1983, I realized that there exists a universal strategy, if you will, for investing in the stock market. It's a methodology designed to keep me and you safely investing the bulk of our money in the market, consistently, with a return on investment that compounds and builds up over time. I wish someone would've told me this decades ago. This universal methodology is made up of four components: market timing, asset allocation, stock selection, and rebalancing.

MARKET TIMING

Multibillionaire Warren Buffett, the incomparable investor nicknamed "The Oracle of Omaha," (he's from Nebraska) is known for his aphorisms, and one of my favorites about his investment strategy is this one:

> *"We simply attempt to be fearful when others are greedy and to be greedy only when others are fearful."*
>
> **—WARREN BUFFET,** 1986 Berkshire Hathaway Chairman's Letter

As an individual investor, you can't time the markets, which is why I'm not an advocate for investing like a trader, though you can learn to recognize greed (also known as irrational exuberance) and fearfulness (also known as panic) and use those as your investment signposts.

You can readily know when we're in a bull market (two or more consecutive quarters of growth) or a bear market (two or more consecutive quarters of contraction). However, you can't know if we're from the bottom of a bear market or the top of a bull market. It's simply impossible to discern. Therefore, since we can't successfully time the market to our advantage, I keep things simple by loading up on stocks under two conditions: when I know for sure that the US economy is in recession, in which case I know I'm not buying stocks at the top of the market, and I can ride the market until it and the price of the stock recovers; or I'll load up on a stock when I'm confident that its price is lower than its intrinsic value. In other words, I believe it's worth more than the current price because of other factors like potential growth, new product development, and so forth.

There is a time to keep money in your safer money market or bond investments, but there's also a time to take your capital out and put it to work for you in riskier asset classes—not without fear, but with courage based upon research. That's how you turn your idle money into smart money. The most important factors in investing are your point of view, your beliefs, your degree of risk tolerance, and your level of courage. Like most folks, I'd love to have the investment savvy of a Goldman Sachs' analyst, but I haven't made the type of lifelong commitment to develop the skills that they have, and I don't expect I ever will.

As tough as it seems to pick a string of stock market winners, it's equally tough to pick a string of losers. That's right. The market is a capricious and unpredictable beast, and it's as hard to determine which assets will rise as it is to know which ones will decline. That's why I advise you to choose your moments to invest with a consistent rhythm rather than waiting for what seems like the exact right time. Think of it this way: if you'd bought Amazon stock when it first went public, you'd have made money hundreds of times over. But if you'd bought it a month or two after it first went public, you'd still have made money hundreds of times over. The same is true if you'd bought it six months after it went public. Whatever interval you'd bought it at, you'd have made a phenomenally handsome return on your investment. Did the person who invested on day one of Amazon's IPO (initial public offering) make a better return than the person who invested six months later? Yes, they did. Does the person who invested six months later wish they'd never invested because they didn't get in at the exact best moment? You can be sure they don't, though maybe we can ask them when they come back from sailing the yacht they bought with all their profit.

See what I'm driving at? I don't want you to wait for the "perfect" moment. I want you to jump in now and start swimming, even if the water feels a little cold at first. You'll get used to it. Pretty soon, by consistently investing, you'll begin to realize the type of long-term returns I've been talking about throughout this book. Like the weather, the market is complex, difficult to predict, and subject to small changes which have big consequences. That's why my advice is to mitigate your risk rather than hope to get lucky.

ASSET ALLOCATION

When it comes to the markets, I'm a conservative guy. I value my hard-earned money, and I hate losing it; that's why I don't gamble with it. What I like to do is put my money to work and be rewarded with a reasonable return. My risk profile can best be expressed in baseball terms: I'm not swinging for the fences; I'm looking for steady base hits with an occasional double up the middle and perhaps a home run every few years. All I care about is winning, not whether someone wants my autograph. Every investor needs to select their asset allocation so that it aligns with their personal risk tolerance and where they are in life. However, there's a critical distinction to be made; if you are late to the wealth-building game and you feel like you've lost too much time, you might think you have to invest in riskier assets to get higher returns. That is categorically wrong and a good way to lose your shirt. The answer in that situation is to invest a greater portion of your income by increasing your savings, adding an income stream or two, and making more money available to you to invest. It's perfectly all right to have a small portion of your investment portfolio in higher-risk assets (as Amazon or Google were, for example, back when they first opened shop) but not the bulk of it.

You'll have to pick or design your own asset allocation model according to your needs. Cash is an asset category too, or what's known as "cash equivalents" like Treasury bills, money market deposit accounts, and so on. These are the safest investments and, unsurprisingly, the ones with the least amount of upside. What's more, cash is subject to inflation, which decreases its value. Some cash or cash equivalents are advisable, though not as a primary investment strategy.

Here are a couple of examples to give you an idea of how allocating assets works. Depending on your risk tolerance, you can select how you want to distribute and diversify your investment portfolio. To pick an asset allocation that aligns with your personal risk tolerance, do some research, and give it a run. Meet with a representative from your brokerage firm for guidance, or seek the advice of your financial planner/adviser.[2]

---

[2] "Investing Ideas for Your IRA," Fidelity, March 7, 2022, https://www.fidelity.com/viewpoints /retirement/ira-portfolio?ccsource=Google.

Ibbotson Associates, 2019
Asset Allocation Models

Choose an investment mix you are comfortable with

	Conservative	Balanced	Growth	Aggressive growth

Legend: US stock, Foreign stock, Bond, Short-term investments

Conservative: 14%, 6%, 30%, 50%
Balanced: 15%, 10%, 35%, 40%
Growth: 5%, 21%, 49%, 25%
Aggressive growth: 15%, 25%, 60%

Annual return

	Conservative	Balanced	Growth	Aggressive growth
Average annual return	5.89%	7.83%	8.80%	9.47%
Worst 12-month return	-17.67%	-40.64%	-52.92%	-60.78%
Best 12-month return	31.06%	76.57%	109.55%	136.07%
Worst 20-year return (annualized)	2.92%	3.43%	3.10%	2.66%
Best 20-year return (annualized)	10.98%	13.83%	15.34%	16.49%
Historical volatility	4.49%	9.54%	13.03%	15.72%

Data source: Ibbotson Associates, 2019 (1926-2018). Past performance is no guarantee of future results. Returns include the reinvestment of dividends and other earnings. This chart is for illustrative purposes only. It is not possible to invest directly in an index. Time periods for best and worst returns are based on calendar year. For information on the indexes used to construct this table, see Data Source in the notes below. The purpose of the target asset mixes is to show how target asset mixes may be created with different risk and return characteristics to help meet an investor's goals. You should choose your own investments based on your particular objectives and situation. Be sure to review your decisions periodically to make sure they are still consistent with your goals.

Merill Lynch Asset Allocation Models

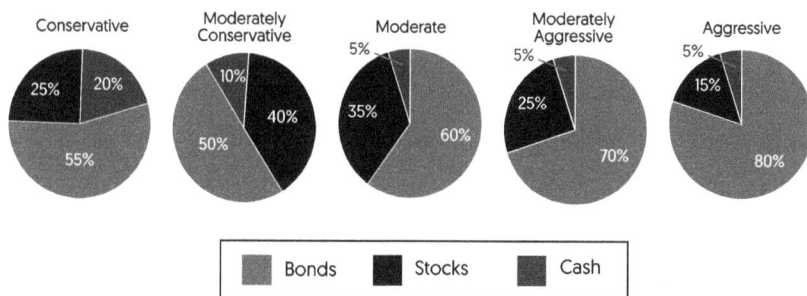

Conservative — 20%, 55%, 25%

Moderately Conservative — 10%, 40%, 50%

Moderate — 5%, 60%, 35%

Moderately Aggressive — 5%, 70%, 25%

Aggressive — 5%, 80%, 15%

Bonds   Stocks   Cash

Source: Bank of America Merrill Lynch Research Investment Committee (RIC) Report March 2011. Models are for illustrative purposes only. Merrill Lynch has changed the allocation of each model in the past and may change the allocations in the future, depending upon research and investment strategy recommendations.

STOCK SELECTION

In my experience, stock selection is the hardest part of securities investing. While estimates vary, there are presently upwards of 5,000 publicly traded stocks on the New York Stock Exchange (NYSE) and the National Association of Securities Dealers Automated Quotations (NASDAQ). Thus, I'd like to recommend a few tried-and-true steps that may help you navigate such a crowded field and set you up as a lifelong securities investor.

Always Be Learning

Spend some time with a brokerage firm, such as Schwab, Fidelity, and TD Ameritrade, to name but a few of them. They offer free classes on learning to invest as well as a host of literature that you can study and learn from. You can also take courses at your local university or community college.

There are also countless books, seminars, and courses offered by private organizations and individuals designed to teach you how to invest intelligently. A note of caution though: always check out the reviews online and try to talk to people who have attended the seminars and courses because, sadly, there are a lot of scam artists out there looking to get rich off you instead of helping you get rich.

Aim High but Start Low

If you're only now getting started with securities investing, consider investing in low-cost index funds. That sage advice comes from none other than Charles Schwab himself. As you continue to learn how to invest, and you begin to feel more comfortable with the risks, you can take more on.

Keep It Simple (K. I. S. S.)

In the Army, we had an acronym we used time and again: K. I. S. S. It stands for Keep It Simple, Stupid. That goes for smart folks like you as well. Don't make your decisions unnecessarily complicated when they don't have to be. Look at it this way: if you wanted to loan some money to one of your friends in hopes of them returning your money plus a little extra money for trusting them, would you choose Friend A, whom you've known and been associated with since you were in Kindergarten, or Friend B, whom you met a few months ago through a referral and whose behavior is unknown (and speculative at best)? Although past performance doesn't dictate future success, at least with Friend A you've seen how they react when things go well and when they go sour. You can much more accurately predict how they will behave.

It's the same for stocks. Would it make sense to put 95–98 percent of your investment cash in the stock of a new sexy tech firm that's only been around for a year? Or would it be safer and wiser to put 95–98 percent of your investment in a company that you've grown up with since you were a child, whose stock has weathered the market's ups and downs time and again yet continues to grow? See what I mean?

I recommend you start by investing 95–98 percent of your investment capital in companies you know, such as Coke, IBM, Google, Disney, or McDonald's, and the remaining 2–5 percent in the shares of speculative companies or investments that you don't yet know well. By that, I mean initial public offering (IPO) companies, crypto currencies, or companies that (based on your research) you believe in but lack the track record of an Apple or Amazon.

I'm not suggesting you buy any specific stocks or investments; these are merely examples of blue-chip companies or investments you are likely to have heard of. Whichever ones you select, I still want you to do your research and read the prospectuses and annual reports of companies or funds you're interested in investing in because, as investors, we must always be looking out for what's going on now *and* what's going to happen next. How has the stock done in the past year or two? Are there any big changes on the horizon (for example, Disney stock recently soared when Disney got into the streaming business with Disney+)? If you're nervous at this point (and if so, that's fine), you can elect to use DCA and buy several "slices" or fractional shares of stock through Charles Schwab, Fidelity, and many other trading platforms. Fractional shares allow you to buy a slice of a company's stock such as Amazon's for as little as five dollars. The point is to start building your confidence to where you can invest at a high level, in a diversified manner, and thereby propel your journey to Destination Millionaire.

As of this writing, the value of all cryptocurrency tokens in circulation sits at $2.6 trillion,[3] indicating a massive cryptocurrency frenzy. This hunger for crypto is taking place despite cryptocurrencies being unregulated, wildly volatile in daily price, and unbacked in valuation by corporate revenues, profits, or balance sheet assets. No matter how you look at it, crypto investing is highly speculative, so be sure to treat it that way by keeping it in that 2–5 percent range of your overall portfolio until it proves itself otherwise.

Go with a Pro

Consider seeking the help of a professional adviser. I discuss in greater detail how to find the right adviser for you later in this chapter. Because the number of choices is so vast, it is not a bad idea to work with an adviser to assist you in making stock selections that align with your asset allocation goals and risk tolerance. Professional advisers have access to a wealth of resources from their firms; they expose you to securities and strategies you may have never heard of or considered. Typically, a professional adviser is a client-facing representative, in this case facing you, though the real magic is happening behind the scenes by the money managers. They are the ones who are glued to their computer screens, reviewing all the research and selecting the stocks that align with each asset allocation model. The financial adviser is the trained salesperson who uses technical information and research conducted by the money managers and traders to create customized portfolios for their clients. So, if you decide to use a

---

[3] Emma Newbery, "There's More Money Than Ever in Cryptocurrencies, but What Does That Mean?" Motley Fool, November 20, 2021, https://www.fool.com/the-ascent/cryptocurrency /articles/theres-more-money-than-ever-in-cryptocurrencies-but-what-does-that-mean/.

professional adviser, stay actively involved and up to date on your investments' performances.

Do Some Homework

Before agreeing to stock purchases that I or anyone else might recommend, spend some time reading and learning about those companies. Make sure you are comfortable about the company's products, reputation, and outlook. If you're using an adviser, ask them for their firm's research; often, a team of money managers publishes their analyses of various stocks and makes it available to their clients at no charge. Do a search on the latest news on the company, including news from the recent past. Do their values align with yours? Are they a socially responsible company? Does that even matter to you? My point is, don't be too hands-off. Use a professional adviser to up your game and improve your knowledge of securities investing.

There are numerous other resources you can use to identify securities in which you may want to invest, such as financial periodicals, online services, or business and finance-related TV shows. *The Wall Street Journal*, *Money Magazine*, *Kiplinger*, and *Forbes* are but a few of the countless publications that offer insights about investment, new companies on the horizon, or investing tips and ideas. TV shows like *Squawk Box*, *Mad Money with Jim Cramer*, CNN's *Your Money*, or online publications like *The Motley Fool* are excellent sources of investing information. The list is almost inexhaustible, but remember, free advice isn't always good advice. No matter which sources you use to help identify and select the securities in your portfolio, do some digging around to ensure each investment meets your goals and risk tolerance level.

REBALANCING: THE GOOD, THE BAD, AND THE UGLY

Every three, six, twelve, or twenty-four months, consider rebalancing the securities in your portfolio to maintain your original asset allocation mix. This is necessary because, over time, some of your investment categories may grow while others will contract, thereby throwing your asset allocation out of alignment with your declared risk tolerance. By rebalancing, you'll ensure that your portfolio does not overemphasize one or more asset categories, and you'll return your portfolio to a comfortable level of risk.

However, I ask that you take this rebalancing advice with a large grain of salt. Over the past thirteen years, we've experienced an unprecedented bull run. Rebalancing during this period would have resulted in missed opportunities on many securities. It all goes back to your risk tolerance and a judgment call you need to make. For example, let's say you've determined that stock investments should represent 60 percent of your portfolio, but after a recent stock market surge, your stock investments have come to represent 80 percent of your portfolio. To properly rebalance, you'd need to either sell some of your stocks or invest in an under-weighted asset category to reestablish your original asset allocation mix (60 percent of your portfolio).

The prevailing recommendation is to rebalance to minimize portfolio losses, but you'll have to decide for yourself when and what securities in your portfolio to hold or sell. The key is to continue to grow your Freedom Fund as safely and as large as you can. Whenever you rebalance, you'll also need to review the investments within each asset allocation category in case any of these investments are underperforming or faced with a less-than-promising outlook. This is your chance to sell them and purchase securities that you have more faith in.

There are essentially three ways you can rebalance your portfolio. You can sell off investments from over-weighted asset categories and use the proceeds to purchase investments for under-weighted asset categories. You can purchase new investments for under-weighted asset categories. Or, if you are making continuous contributions to the portfolio, you can alter your contributions so that more investments go to under-weighted asset categories until your portfolio is back into balance.

Rebalancing can be complicated and, thus, another area where having a professional financial adviser may help significantly. They have the tools and resources to rebalance your portfolio much more easily than you can on your own. Before you rebalance your portfolio, remember to consider whether the method of rebalancing you decide to use will trigger transaction fees or tax consequences. For instance, any securities sold for a profit within a year of their purchase will require you to pay short-term capital gains or ordinary income taxes (both of which are higher than long-term capital gains taxes imposed on securities sold after a year and one day). Your financial professional or tax adviser can help you identify ways that you can minimize any of these potential costs.

HIRING A FINANCIAL ADVISER

Now that you have a methodology for building and maintaining an investment portfolio, you can more clearly see how the tasks of managing that portfolio can become a full-time job on its own. So, if you do go the route of hiring a professional adviser, here are some guidelines to consider in your search for the right person for you and your needs.

I believe the best way to find a financial adviser or financial planner is through referral. I will only use advisers or planners who are referred to me by millionaires who value their money as much as, or more, than I do mine. Before you select an adviser from the barrage of marketing material that's likely to get sent your way, look around in your own network first. Is there someone you know who is dead serious about their money? Find out if they are using an adviser, and if so, how long they have been working with that adviser. Ask what type of average annual returns they have realized while working with their adviser. Have the returns been higher than the fees or commissions paid to the adviser? Would they recommend that person to you? What did they like or dislike about their adviser? What percentage are they paying in fees? Is the adviser compensated via commission or a percentage of invested capital? In other words, don't just skim the surface in this process; go deep.

But don't stop there. Go even deeper and ask the toughest questions. I want to know if my financial adviser is achieving their own financial goals. My philosophy is this: how can you advise me on how to manage my money, if you're doing a poor job managing your own money? If your financial adviser avoids answering those kinds of questions or admits that his financial house is not in order, or if he gives you a moving heartfelt explanation as to why things haven't worked out, smile politely, and then run!

There are also several online tools that can help match you with financial advisers near you, such as Smart Asset. The Association of African American Financial Advisors is also an excellent resource: https://www.aaafainc.com/. Do some investigating, pose tough questions, ask for references, and then go with the adviser you feel is right for you. You'll need to constantly monitor your finances to make sure your adviser is doing right by you. If you're still concerned, run a background check on them to make sure there are no pending lawsuits or fraud-related cases against them.

HOW MUCH DOES IT COST TO WORK WITH
A FINANCIAL ADVISER?

A financial adviser or financial planner are broad terms that encompass several different types of professionals. For instance, one type of adviser might help you develop a financial plan, budgets, or plan your retirement, including helping you create and manage your stock and bond investment portfolio. Another type of adviser can help you with tax and estate planning or assist you in developing a financial plan to help cover your children's college expenses. The list goes on.

When it comes to compensating financial advisers, there are essentially three ways in which they collect their fees: on a flat-fee basis, on a commissions basis, or as a percentage of your total assets they have under management. Understandably, the less money your adviser is managing for you, the more likely it is that they'll charge a flat fee. Flat fee advisers appear to be more expensive, largely because a flat fee doesn't incentivize them to help you grow your assets. They have no skin in your game. A financial planner who charges a percentage of your portfolio, on the other hand, makes money as your portfolio grows—a nice incentive for both you and them. Also, the more money of yours they manage, the lower the percentage they are likely to charge overall (typically anywhere from 0.25–2 percent). The one potential disadvantage of an adviser who charges a percentage is that they'll probably have a minimum requirement in terms of the amount of your money they manage to make it worth their while. So, you may have to at least start with an adviser who works on a flat-fee basis or a commission-based adviser who gets paid based on the products they sell you: insurance policies, stocks, and so forth.

The fees charged by these professionals are not insignificant, so a good rule of thumb is to insist upon a minimum annual yield of 5–7 percent, after they've deducted their fee. Their advice should be making you money, not making you cash poor. Since using a financial adviser doesn't eliminate brokerage fees either, be sure to include those costs in determining if working with a financial adviser is the right thing for you. If by using an adviser you're not realizing a 5–7 percent return on your invested capital, you might want to search around for an adviser who can get your money performing at that level.

Above all, remember this: your financial adviser has a fiduciary duty to work in your best interests, to carefully vet any product or service before recommending it to you, to execute financial transactions on your behalf at the most opportune time allowable, and to disclose any conflict of interest at all that they may be a party to. All investment advisers registered with the US Securities and Exchange Commission (SEC) or a state securities regulator must act as fiduciaries. On the other hand, broker-dealers, stockbrokers, and insurance agents are only required to fulfill a suitability obligation, which means they do not have to place your interests above their own (as required of fiduciaries); they only must sell you investments that seem suitable to your interests. Big difference.

7 STEPS TO BECOMING A MILLIONAIRE BY INVESTING IN SECURITIES

Step One—Open a brokerage account at one of the major brokerage firms (Charles Schwab, Fidelity, TD Ameritrade, E*Trade, Ameritrade, Merrill Edge, etc.). At some firms, you can open an account with as little as $0, with no fees, so there is no reason why you cannot open an account today.

Step Two—Review your M$M Power Budget and M$M Master Plan to determine how much investment money (capital) you can draw from every paycheck or existing investment profits. How much more are you saving by making Millionaire Money Moves—earning more with your side hustle and paying and consuming less?

Step Three—Select an asset allocation that suits your risk tolerance, whether it is conservative, aimed at moderate growth, or aggressive. Remember to invest only 2–5 percent of your portfolio in speculative companies or investments and 95 percent in companies that you know, trust, and believe in for the long haul.

Step Four—Create a diversified investment portfolio of twenty to thirty securities or index funds and ETFs across a variety of industries (tech, healthcare, insurance, manufacturing, retail, international, etc.) by researching and determining the securities (stocks, index funds, mutual funds, ETFs, bonds, and commodities) that align with your selected asset allocation. Research potential securities through periodicals, online tools, TV programs, and/or an adviser.

Step Five—Spread your investment capital across your portfolio of securities and be sure they align with your asset allocation. Every two to four weeks, purchase securities (stocks, index funds, mutual funds, ETFs, bonds, and commodities) across your portfolio. This should be done monthly for the rest of your life.

Step Six—Rebalance your portfolio every six to twelve months (plus one day, so annual short-term gains become long-term ones) to maintain your diversification and minimize your risk. Add more securities to your portfolio as you learn and earn more money. If you adhere to your selected, diversified asset allocation, you should be fine. It's perfectly okay to switch your asset allocation model as you age or as your life changes, but always remember you may have to pay short- or long-term capital gains taxes on your gains depending on how long you hold on to your securities.

Step Seven—As you earn more income, invest more capital consistently across your entire portfolio until you achieve your desired endgame or Freedom Fund balance. If you've earned enough, extend your diversification by investing in capital-intensive categories like real estate, entrepreneurship, or alternative investments (angel investing, venture capital investing, or private equity).

This will all take care, patience, and time, but if you're consistent about it, you will achieve Destination Millionaire and beyond in time.

INVESTING IN REAL ESTATE

REAL ESTATE INVESTING INCLUDES BUYING HOUSES, APART-
ments, strip malls, office buildings, warehouses, factories, or land. It's my
personal favorite as an investment category and as you'll see, it's also ideally suited to your wealth-building journey because the need for housing
and space grows constantly over time. That makes real estate investment
generally stable, with price appreciation and income benefits that last for
as long as you own your property. What's more, since you can increase
the rents on your properties by 3–5 percent or more per year, you've got
a perfect hedge against inflation built right into your investment. You
can even leverage your property by using some of its equity to buy more
property and, thereby, create further income for yourself. What's not to
like? (Well, a few things, but we'll get into that later.)

As you've likely seen firsthand, property values tend to go up over
time, which means the properties themselves are typically able to generate
sustainable income for life. Luckily, the initial challenges of managing and
stabilizing a property diminish over time as you continue to learn the

ropes and work out the kinks of a property. After a while it all becomes smooth sailing.

What I particularly like is how the income I receive through real estate is passive, and the taxes I pay on the income are lowered through depreciation. In other words, I can begin deducting a portion of the purchase price and improvements of a building or a unit from my taxes, right from the time I rent it out or "place it in service" as it's legally called. At the current depreciation rate of approximately 3.5 percent per year, that means in about twenty-seven and a half years, I'll have been able to deduct the entire price from my tax bill. That's my kind of gravy!

As I mentioned, while there are a host of excellent benefits to real estate investment, like any other endeavor, there's no such thing as a free lunch. You must be able to afford the monthly payments on any mortgage you take on. Being a landlord is challenging, time consuming, and often costly. Maintaining your properties takes time and money, and if you are working a nine-to-five job, it's difficult to keep up with the demands of being a landlord. Real estate is also not the quickest investment performer, and it can take five, ten, fifteen, or even twenty-plus years before a property appreciates in value.

Therefore, although I love investing in real estate, I don't do it to the exclusion of the explosive opportunities available in securities investing—nor should you. I like to think of them as thunder and lightning; real estate appreciates at the speed of sound, while securities can add value at the speed of light. The smart move is to have a balanced portfolio by investing in both. And because there are so many nuances to real estate investment, far too many to cover here, I'm going to focus on introducing you to the types of real estate you can invest in and the acquisition requirements you'll face. I'll also highlight some of the pros and cons and investment strategies, and

I'll show you how I analyze real estate deals. This will provide you with the foundation of a real estate education and portfolio to build on from here on into the future.

A couple of key terms I'll be using merit further explanation before we dive in. Whenever I refer to what's called "equity," I mean the anticipated amount of money left over from a property after the debt on it is paid. For example, if your apartment was worth $150,000 when you bought it, and you borrowed $100,000 from the bank to purchase it, your equity on the day of purchase would have been $50,000 (minus realtor fees, taxes, and closing costs you would incur had you sold it immediately). A year later, assuming you'd made your mortgage payments and thus lowered the overall debt by, say, $6,000, then your total equity would increase to $56,000, *assuming the apartment was still worth $150,000.* Any amount that the value of the apartment appreciated would add even more to your equity; conversely, any amount that the value depreciated would subtract from your equity.

The second term I'll be using is "investment property." That simply means a property that you buy but don't personally use; instead, you rent it out to others. There are cases of investment properties that you partially use (such as a summer home that you rent out to others, though you spend a couple weeks in it in the off seasons). But for our purposes, we'll focus primarily on properties used solely for investment purposes.

The most common types of real estate you can invest in are as follows:

SINGLE-FAMILY HOME

This refers to a stand-alone home that doesn't share any walls with another home. A single-family residence also sits on its own parcel of land, has one kitchen, dedicated utilities, and its own private street access. Condos, townhomes, and co-ops also fall in the category of single-family homes. Single-family homes can be used by an owner to live in or considered an investment if they're rented to a long-term or short-term vacation tenant (such as an Airbnb guest). These are commonly referred to as vacation rentals.

DUPLEXES, TRIPLEXES, AND FOURPLEXES

A duplex, triplex, or fourplex is a multi-family home that has two, three, or four units in the same building or on the same plot of land. These units always share a common wall, but their floor plans can vary. They can be arranged side by side or stacked on top of one another, each one occupying an entire floor or two of the building. The main advantage of investing in these types of complexes is that if the owner occupies the property, the lending requirements are like that of purchasing a single-family home, and thus, the investor can put down as little as 3 percent of the purchase price to qualify. Additionally, the income from the remaining one to three units will contribute to the owner's income when calculating the purchaser's debt-to-income ratios (see an explanation of DTI ratio below).

COMMERCIAL

Commercial real estate (CRE) is property used exclusively for business-related purposes, or to provide a workspace rather than a living space. Most often, commercial real estate is leased to tenants to conduct income-generating activities. This broad category of real estate can include everything from a single storefront to a huge shopping center, hotels, restaurants, and healthcare facilities. There are, in turn, five types of commercial real estate:

Residential Multi-Family

An apartment building which contains *more* than four units under one roof is considered a commercial property. This includes more than one building of that size (or greater) on a single land complex.

Mixed-Use

Mixed-use commercial property is either a building or a land development that includes both residential and commercial space. For example, a structure that has office or retail space on the ground floor and apartment units on the top floor would be considered mixed-use because it contains residential and office/retail space.

Retail Property

This encompasses individual storefronts as well as retail shopping centers and may include ancillary uses such as office space, medical suites, or food services like a restaurant or bar.

Office Building

A building that provides space suitable for clerical, administrative, or medical business operations.

Industrial

This category is for warehouses or factories designed to manufacture, store, and distribute goods.

LAND

Land purchases include anything that is naturally attached to the property, such as plants, boulders, minerals, or any substances that lie below the earth's surface (such as oil). It also includes the air space, although how much of that air space is yours to exploit is subject to local regulations. You can think of land as a combination of its surface, subsurface below ground, and air space above.

REAL ESTATE INVESTMENT TRUSTS (REITS)

These are securities that exclusively invest in real estate. We won't be covering REIT investment here, but if the thought of being a landlord makes you queasy, you may want to have a look at REIT investment instead.

Don't worry; there won't be a quiz on all these items at the end of this chapter, though do take a moment to familiarize yourself with each category as we explore the best ways to turn each of these investments into lasting wealth.

REAL ESTATE ACQUISITION
REQUIREMENTS

As you can see in the M$M Investment Ladder ((Sub) Chapter 7.6 on Investing), you'll need to get your capital to at least Level 3 to begin investing in real estate. At that point you can consider purchasing single-family properties (e.g., detached homes, condominiums, co-ops, or townhouses). There are a series of acquisition requirements that go along with purchasing real estate, including the down payment, closing costs, and any inspection costs needed to evaluate whether a property is worth purchasing. Depending on the type of real estate you're purchasing, the acquisition requirements can vary.

Let's look at each of these acquisition requirements individually.

DOWN PAYMENT

Residential properties require anywhere from 3 percent to 20 percent down, depending on the size of the loan and the price of the property. For traditional residential purchases, banks typically prefer to loan 90 percent of the value of the home, thus requiring you to put down the remaining 10 percent of the purchase price. Jumbo loans are what are known as non-conforming loans, which presently means that—depending on the state in which you are making the purchase—the loan limit exceeds $558,000. Jumbo loans normally require a 20 percent down payment.

Before forking over money for a sizable down payment and closing costs, it pays to contact the local housing office where you're looking to buy because many municipalities have down payment and closing cost assistance for first-time home buyers based on your family size and income. These assistance programs are offered to purchasers of single-family residences, duplexes, triplexes, and fourplexes if you intend to live in one or more of the units as well.

If you're purchasing a single-family home, duplex, triplex, or fourplex purely for investment purposes, with no intentions of residing in the property, be prepared to put down 20 percent of the contract price as a down payment.

Commercial purchases require a 25–30 percent down payment, or more, depending on the valuation of the property and your financial profile. Banks typically only want to be invested in commercial properties at about 70–75 percent of their appraised value. If you're planning to make significant improvements to the property and need additional funding from a bank, you will likely need to come up with a lot more cash to make that deal happen. The bank will likely want to maintain its 70–75 percent stake in the projected property value even after renovations are considered. If you're short on cash, this is where additional equity investors can help save the day. However, there are many complex nuances to taking on real estate partners that you will need to research on your own.

DEBT-TO-INCOME (DTI) RATIO

This is a fancy acronym used to explain what percentage of your income goes toward your debts each month, although its scope goes even further. It also includes your rent(s) collected as income and any recurring payments you have, such as child support or alimony. Lenders use DTI to determine how risky it is to lend to you. Usually, they require a maximum of 28 percent on the front end (mortgage expense only) and 36 percent on the back end (mortgage plus your debt-related expenses). Depending on your credit score, you can sometimes exceed those limits, though you'll have to discuss and work that out with your individual mortgage provider.

DTI is also used in multi-family, commercial real estate, except that 75 percent of the income the property is earning gets added to your income. A portion rather than the whole amount is used because it's assumed that not every tenant will pay on time 100 percent of the time. So, if you're able to qualify with a portion of the income, then it's highly likely you can afford to continue making mortgage payments even during tough periods.

CREDIT REQUIREMENTS

Your credit score gives lenders a sense of how consistent you are at paying your bills on time and how much you value borrowed money. Your credit score needs to average 620 or higher across three major credit agencies to purchase single-family, duplexes, triplexes, and fourplexes. However, because each lender has different credit score guidelines, you may be able to qualify with a lower credit score.

Purchasing commercial real estate typically requires a credit score above 700 due to the risks associated with owning and managing commercial real estate. Lenders want to make absolutely sure that you have the wherewithal to weather any potential storm that could come your way as a commercial real estate investor. Furthermore, with you having a 700 or higher credit score, the lender can feel confident that you have or can readily secure alternative capital if the need suddenly arises.

CLOSING COSTS

At the time you purchase your property, you must plan to have 3 percent above the purchase price available in cash, to cover closing costs. That includes items like inspection and appraisal fees, deed recording fees, loan processing fees, legal fees, title insurance fees, transfer and property taxes, escrow fees, and a whole host of others. Although these fees are a normal part of a real estate transaction, they add up in a hurry. The point is to plan on having that extra cash ready; 3 percent should cover single-family or dwellings as large as fourplexes.

When investing in commercial real estate or land, closing and acquisition costs are significantly higher. Often the legal fees (for your attorney to draft or review the sales contract) plus the inspection and appraisal fees can be as much as $20,000 or more, depending on the property, even before you finally decide to go ahead with the purchase. If anything alarming is discovered during inspection, you can end up having to walk away from the thousands of dollars you've spent to have the property evaluated. This is one reason why you must get your capital up high enough before venturing into commercial real estate investment.

CASH RESERVES

Many lenders require you to keep some additional funds in cash as well. One or two months' mortgage payment in reserve is usually required for residential properties, though this amount can vary depending on your lender. You may need six months to one year of cash reserve to acquire certain commercial properties. Make sure you find out the requirements of your lender in advance and then be prepared to do what's required; otherwise, you risk wasting time and money on inspection, appraisal, and/or legal fees.

I realize some of these requirements sound daunting. For most folks, the first and largest real estate transaction they make is buying their own home. Take comfort that there are millions of people out there who have managed to navigate this process at least one time. Once you get through your first real estate transaction, you'll feel a lot more confident, knowledgeable, and ready for all the deals you'll be making down the road.

Before I get into some of the pros and cons of real estate investing, I want to clarify how loans and interest rates work. You'll almost certainly be using some leverage (the pros call it "borrowed money") to finance your investments, so let's be sure we understand the nuances before we sign on any dotted lines.

INTEREST RATES AND LOAN TERMS
(FIXED VERSUS VARIABLE)

Interest rates on mortgages are either fixed for the entire loan term (usually fifteen or thirty years) or variable based on the fluctuations of the mortgage market. Do you remember how, back in *Why Should White Guys Have All the Wealth?* in (Sub) Chapter 7.4, I showed you how even a slight variation in your monthly mortgage payment could add up to a lot of money over time? That's why banks offer you the option of setting the interest rate on your loan now or leaving it up to chance in the hope that the rate will go lower. Banks don't care which one you choose because they still make their money. However, they'll offer you a lower interest rate initially for a variable mortgage because, if the rates go up in the future, they'll make even more money from you than they would have if you settled on a fixed rate. You may have good reason to take on that risk (for example, if you're planning to flip a property in a year or two). It may make sense not to worry too much about inflation over such a short period of time. Your choice depends on your situation and your risk profile. Do you want to be exposed to inflation (which drives interest rates up), or would you rather get a lower rate now and take on that risk?

Commercial properties work differently. They typically have a fixed interest rate for twenty-five years, which is then adjusted every five years until the loan is paid off. Interest rates for commercial properties tend to be higher than residential ones because they are seen by lenders as riskier investments. Commercial properties typically have a twenty-five-year term, which means you're expected to pay off the property in twenty-five years instead of thirty years for residential.

Beyond fixed and variable rates, there are other structural differences among loans. For instance, on most mortgages, you pay part of the overall interest and part of the principal amount you borrowed each time you make a payment. However, some loans are interest only, whereby the principal never gets reduced until all the interest is paid off first.

If you get into trouble due to rising interest rates, or if you're looking to save money due to falling interest rates, refinancing is a great strategy to lower your costs and increase your profits. Refinancing may require you to pay some money up front (known as "points"), though over the long haul you will save significantly more than the points you pay. A good rule of thumb is to refinance whenever interest rates go down by 1 percent or more. At that point, many folks reset the payoff terms back to twenty-five or thirty years, though I personally prefer having my properties paid off at the end of the original loan term. That's why when I refinance a property, I usually keep the terms set at their original payoff date. This is a personal choice you'll have to make based on where you are and where you want to be financially.

WHAT ARE THE PROS AND CONS OF INVESTING IN REAL ESTATE?

As with any investment strategy, you must accept the good with the bad. Here are some salient factors to keep in mind in the world of real estate investment:

INVESTING IN SINGLE-FAMILY PROPERTIES

Let's begin with the good. You can purchase a lot of value while only having to invest 3–10 percent of the total cost. That value can appreciate significantly over time. You can borrow money against the equity of your investment to fund other investments, and you can increase rents to stay ahead of inflation. What's not to love, right?

Well, a few things. With single-family properties in particular, values can vary widely because they're based on comparable sales, market demand, and supply. If you decide to live in your property, you can't derive any income from it. Borrowing against equity increases your overall debt, and even one vacancy can have a significant impact on your ability to make your mortgage payments. Lastly, the more properties you purchase results in more maintenance and upkeep that need to be done on them (multiple lawns to cut, multiple roofs to service, entire houses to paint, multiple locations to service, etc.).

COMMERCIAL INVESTING

When it comes to commercial real estate investing, the pros and cons change quite a bit. On the plus side, owning a property offers sustainable income and appreciation for as long as you own it. There is a huge demand for multi-family properties and certain commercial properties, such as strip malls, which means they typically sell quickly for a premium. As with commercial office and mixed-use properties, rent increases can always keep you ahead of inflation because businesses can afford higher increases. Similarly, you can borrow against the equity to invest in more assets that appreciate and create further income.

Unlike single-family real estate, having one vacancy shouldn't impact your ability to financially maintain the property because you'll have income from multiple tenants. In addition, the insurance, taxes, maintenance, and repair costs for commercial office buildings, retail centers, and industrial properties are shared by the tenants proportionally (pro rata). This will save you a lot of money as long as you keep your building occupied.

There are a lot of deep-pocketed investors, such as syndicated investor groups, insurance companies, private equity groups, and hedge funds, who purchase large, multi-unit properties, which means your pool of potential buyers is large and constantly replenishing itself. The value of a commercial property is based on income, something called Cap Rate (i.e., the ratio between the net operating income produced by an asset and its sales price), and to a lesser degree on comparable sales. Thus, if your rents are high and you're making good income, the high demand for your property will drive up the value of your property.

Now for the flip side. As you may have surmised, given the size of these properties, the costs of property management, repair, and maintenance are high, and the work is demanding. It often requires a professional staff. Unsurprisingly, owners of these properties sometimes neglect to update them when they should. But avoiding maintenance or providing bad customer service risks losing good tenants. Even if you're able to cash in on a great price to buy a property that's failed to update, the capital expenditures (Cap X) required to do the updates can be huge. Also, since large, multi-family and commercial properties are often purchased by syndicated investor groups, private equity groups, insurance companies, and deep-pocketed hedge funds, it's frequently difficult for an individual investor like you to find deals.

INVESTING IN LAND

When it comes to land investment, there is an entirely different set of pros and cons to consider. This time, I'll start with a few of the shortcomings. It's difficult to borrow money against undeveloped land because the true value of the land is hard to determine. In essence, you're borrowing against the land and its potential; not always an easy sale to a bank, nor to a potential buyer for that matter. The so-called carrying costs of land (property taxes, interest payments, association dues, etc.) can be prohibitive, especially if you're not deriving any income from the land itself. Construction costs alone sometimes outstrip what would be the cost of renovating an existing building because you need to do site engineering, mechanical engineering, and architectural plans, and then pay material costs, which are subject to inflation and supply chain scarcity (the COVID-19-related spike in lumber prices is a good example of what can happen).

Conversely, you can create, design, and build whatever you want (subject to local zoning regulations). Whatever you build will be new and under warranty, which means your maintenance and repair costs will be lower and likely deferred, as compared to those of an existing structure. There's also a chance that the land, if bought in an "up and coming" area, may skyrocket in price before you even get around to building anything, especially if another developer needs your land for their project. The same is true of air rights, particularly in big cities like New York or San Francisco. Perhaps there's even a windfall lying below the surface of land you may purchase. Los Angeles, for one, is filled with landowners who derive income from oil reserves that were discovered miles below the surface, long after they purchased the land above it.

FOUR MONEY-MAKING STRATEGIES TO USE IN REAL ESTATE INVESTMENT

In my twenty-plus years of real estate investing, I've come to believe there are four reliable ways to make money in real estate investment: buying into a buyer's market and selling into a seller's market (a.k.a. buy low and sell high); buying and holding properties for long-term income and appreciation; buying upscale properties and upselling them at a far higher price; or buying properties and flipping them for capital appreciation. Each strategy has its own nuances, and the first strategy is also applicable to the three others. Let's take a closer look.

BUY IN A BUYER'S MARKET, SELL IN A SELLER'S MARKET

No matter what type of purchase you make, *when* you purchase and sell your properties is as important as *what* you purchase. The classic advice is to "buy low, sell high," though in real estate, that's also a function of the marketplace itself. I use two indicators to determine when to buy and two different ones to know when it's best to sell. Unlike other forms of investment, you make your money in real estate when you buy it, for the right price, at the moment you buy. Let me explain. You don't realize your profit until you sell, meaning you don't pocket your earnings till then, but when you buy at a good time and price, you've already made money because you've successfully purchased an undervalued asset at its reduced value rather than its true value.

When to Buy

A buyer's market means that the overall real estate market favors the purchaser, not the seller. A buyer's market is in effect whenever housing inventories—meaning the time it takes to sell off the supply of available houses—exceeds seven months. As such, prices and demand are typically lower, and homeowners are more willing to negotiate a lower price to sell their homes.

The ideal time to buy is whenever we're in a buyer's market *and* the economy is in a prolonged or deep recession (a recession is when the economy is down for two consecutive quarters, equal to six months). The Federal Reserve Economic Data tracks the housing supply and provides the inventory calculation on their website: https://fred.stlouisfed.org/series/MSACSR#. Since the economy may still be growing even when the housing supply is greater than seven months, these two indices are not necessarily dependent upon each other.

Another solid indicator of a buyer's market is a proliferation of For Sale signs in people's front yards. As time goes by, if you notice that the signs are still there and the prices for the properties they advertise are being reduced, this is your cue that a buyer's market is afoot. As a rule, the longer it takes to sell a property, the more a seller will be forced to lower their price, especially a buyer who may have already bought another house or needs to move elsewhere for work or for personal reasons.

Keep in mind that you must be willing to be a contrarian to find a great deal on a property. You've got to go against the grain. It took me a long while and a couple of real estate losses to realize this, and I can't tell you how much I wish I'd understood it sooner. When prices are rising in any investment category, especially real estate, it's easy to get caught up in the exuberance of what others are doing. Too often folks enter the market because their friends, family, gardener, or shoeshine guy are bragging about buying a house. They think, "If others can afford a house, then I need to be buying one too." The result is that they overpay. When I see everybody and their mother talking about buying a house, I break out my tent and sleeping bag, investment-wise. You know when folks whose income you question can buy a house? That's an indication that we're headed towards the top of the market. At the top of the market, the banks get mad creative and offer all types of relaxed qualifications programs to get more buyers in. At the same time, if interest rates are low, would-be buyers tend to focus exclusively on how low their payments will be, while failing to pay enough attention to how high the house's price is.

The aftermath of that type of exuberant behavior can be devastating. Take the subprime lending extravaganza of 2005–2006. Bankers were giving out loans like hotcakes. The result: tens of thousands of foreclosed homes, especially in Black neighborhoods. Tens of thousands of African Americans were stripped of their wealth; a bitter and painful collapse I witnessed firsthand. I live in the wealthiest African American county in the country, and it happened here in a big way. The homes my Black neighbors and friends lost ended up in the hands of house flippers who made out like fat cats when the houses either went into foreclosure or had to be unloaded for far below their normal market value. That's why it's so important to know the difference between a false buyer's decisions based on foolishness and a true buyer's market based on data and strategy.

When to Hold

When housing inventories represent a five-to-seven-month supply, the market is considered balanced, favoring neither the buyer nor the seller. During these times, it is most advantageous to hold steady and not buy or sell, except in one of those rare instances where you find an extraordinary opportunity (foreclosure, auction, or divorce sale) and you're confident the property is being sold significantly below its value.

When to Sell

The time to sell real estate, as you've probably deduced, is in a seller's market. A seller's market is when housing inventories are significantly less than a five-month supply, and the economy is in a growth business cycle. A recent example of a seller's market was in 2020 when the housing supply reached three to four months, prior to the coronavirus pandemic. Sale prices approached or exceeded all-time highs because the stock market was booming, interest rates were historically low, and housing inventory was way down. It was a perfect time to sell.

As you learn to recognize the signs of a buyer's or seller's market, it is vital that you amass and hold onto cash reserves, so you can take advantage of the right market when it strikes. That's what making Millionaire Money Moves is all about. As the old joke goes, when your ship comes in, you don't want to be at the airport. Get "lucky" by being well-prepared for fortuitous circumstances like a buyer's or seller's market. My goal is to help you learn this lesson sooner in your investment career instead of later, as I unfortunately did. I also hope you'll have the courage to keep buying even if you make a mistake and buy or sell in the wrong markets. Persistence, not perfection, is the only way to get on the right side of the buying and selling cycle and to learn its ins and outs.

This buying and selling strategy should be part of any of your real estate transactions, including the strategies which are about to follow. Remember this: timing is always everything!

BUY-AND-HOLD FOR LONG-TERM APPRECIATION

If you're specifically looking to generate consistent income through your real estate investments, you can purchase a property, operate it, and increase your rents annually. This strategy in real estate investment is called buy-and-hold. As you simultaneously optimize your expenses, your income will increase even further. A typical rent increase for residential units, depending on the area, is 3–5 percent per year. Commercial rents are different, in that they increase based on the location, quality, and demand for space in the specific property.

In the first instance, as your rents increase, the value of your property increases along with it. Why? Because buyers price a building based on the net rental income it yields. The more money an asset makes, the more valuable it becomes. In commercial real estate, there is also something called "triple net properties" (NNN), which are specifically purchased for the consistent income they generate. NNNs are commonly used for commercial retail, warehouses, and industrial properties. The tenant, rather than the landlord, is responsible for all the build-out costs, maintenance, repairs, pro rata property taxes, insurance, and utilities. Examples of triple net lease tenants would be Starbucks or the United States Postal Service. I have a USPS in one of my buildings, the same building they've rented for over eighty years. When you have a triple net tenant you are essentially receiving the rents as pure income without the cost of expenses because all the expenses to operate the property are paid for by the tenants.

The real opportunity to make money in real estate using the buy-and-hold strategy is when you can find the right type of property in an undesirable area for which there is a major development plan. If you're able to successfully purchase property in a depressed location close to downtown, with high walkability, and near to attractive water features or convenient transportation to major employment areas, the question then becomes how long must you hold before the plan goes into effect and things change? Can you break even or create positive cash flow long enough for the area to take off? It often takes many years, and even decades, before depressed neighborhoods turn around.

I employed this strategy on a property in Jersey City, New Jersey, where I purchased a mixed-use building on a double lot for $360,000 in 2003. Eighteen years later, that section of town is booming, and everyone wants to live there because it's more affordable than other desirable areas nearby. Builders are constructing class-A high rises with rents that are about half of what they are only five minutes drive from the waterfront areas of Jersey City. The land my building sits on is presently worth $2 million, so sometime soon, I plan to tear down the existing building and construct one of my salon studios businesses on the first floor, a twelve-unit apartment building, and a rooftop apartment for myself.

How did I know this turnaround would happen one day? Did I have a crystal ball or Midas touch? Of course not. I did my research. When the city quickly built up the area I was living in and created a light rail train system, I simply followed the train stops. I knew that the other areas would soon follow in terms of development, so I picked an area three short stops away from my condo that was close to the water, close to a national park, close to New York City, five walkable blocks from the light rail, and in an area with low-end retail or none at all (making the five-story building I plan to erect an ideal place for a café, beauty salon, or any type of retail business some day).

One daunting challenge with this strategy, however, is dealing with vacancies. Properties in depressed areas are difficult to lease because only folks familiar and comfortable with the neighborhood will rent in your location. You can't simply put an ad on Zillow.com or Rent.com and expect your email to light up with inquiries. I've found that the best way to find tenants in a depressed area is by putting a "For Rent" sign on the building, speaking to a realtor who's specialized in that neighborhood, and seeking out a referral from an existing good tenant or neighbor. I've even had success renting out to low-income tenants with government subsidies (a.k.a. Section 8), until the neighborhood improved, though in some cases, the neighborhoods where I purchased were initially so bad that even Section 8 tenants didn't want to live there.

In my experience, Section 8 has been a good partner but not an easy one. They have upped their standards of late, which is good for all parties. They inspect every apartment before approving one for their tenant. They make sure that landlords provide a safe and clean space for their clients. They have become very thorough, which is good news for well-meaning landlords, and they pay on time every month. The trade-off is that you must be willing to keep your buildings properly maintained and functioning until the market in the depressed area comes around. At times, you'll doubt yourself and think that the neighborhood will never turn. You may even feel foolish for buying and trying to hold on. But if you carefully focus on the key value factors of a neighborhood (closeness to water, walkability to town, retail, jobs, and major transportation hubs), it will only be a matter of time before things turn in your favor. When neighborhood circumstances turn around, as they have time and again through history, you'll look like a genius, and everyone else will want your property.

Here's a real-life story you can draw inspiration from. Back in the mid-1980s, Federal Express delivered all over the country as they do today, but they refused to deliver packages to the Bedford-Stuyvesant section of Brooklyn because it was deemed too dangerous. Thankfully, a local politician was eventually able to get FedEx to end that policy, and in time, the neighborhood changed too. Today, the biggest risk a FedEx carrier runs in Bed-Stuy is probably overpaying for a tasty, locally made cappuccino. It took twenty-odd years for things to turn around like that, but turn around they did. For folks who were savvy enough to buy-and-hold in that area, it became a real estate lesson in how to become a millionaire starting from the bottom.

BUY UPSCALE, IMPROVE, AND UPSELL OR UPRENT

The third reliable way I've found is to buy properties that are already located in a premium area and invest more money to make them even more premium, while spending significant marketing dollars on them as well. Investors who employ this strategy typically have strong marketing teams that are experts at hyping properties and selling them or renting them for above-market prices. Clearly, this is a risky strategy for the average investor. Most of us don't have the marketing skills, time, or financial resources. This method is most used by big-time developers, including a certain former President and his son-in-law. Make no mistake; it is far easier to make money when you have unlimited funds to invest. The rich get richer than the poor, not because they're smarter, but because they're already rich and thus have more time and resources to investigate and carry out investments. There's never a guarantee that a high-priced investment will pay off.

BUY-AND-FLIP

Flipping properties, whether residential or commercial, is another sound way to make money investing in real estate. The objective of this approach is to grow the capital invested as quickly and as abundantly as possible. When you purchase an investment property to flip, you are putting down anywhere from 25–100 percent (in the case of foreclosures and short-sale properties), plus appraisal, inspection, and attorney's fees. Often, smaller buy-and-flip investors rely on hard money lenders, who then become the primary lien holder of the property to the tune of 60 percent of the property's current value. Hard money lenders usually charge fees for an attorney to prepare the necessary paperwork, a 3 percent (or more) loan origination fee, and 10 percent (or more) in annual interest, to be paid monthly.

The buy-and-flip strategy aims to recoup all the acquisition capital, carrying costs, and renovation costs for the property, as well as to realize a 25 percent or higher return sometime soon. That can be as early as six months on a residential flip to five years on a commercial flip. The secret to successful residential flipping is to buy properties well below market price and make strategic improvements to each property so that you can sell it at a significantly higher price. The secret to successful commercial flipping is to buy properties at or below market price, make strategic improvements to each unit or apartment, and aggressively increase rents for five years before selling it at a significantly higher price. Note how I said "strategic" improvements? Whatever is done to the flip property needs to have your end goal in mind, as opposed to your personal aesthetics or needs. What matters is not so much what you like; it's what sells in the area where your property is located.

While flipping does lead to faster profits, you must be sure to investigate —in advance—the carrying costs (insurance, property taxes, utilities, Homeowners Association fees, etc.) you must pay while renovating the property and any exposure you may have to long- or short-term capital gains taxes, which may erode your profit margin. Be careful, and do your homework, so you don't end up taking a loss.

HOW TO FIND INVESTMENT PROPERTIES

There are five principal sources for locating investment properties to purchase:

1. Private online databases
2. Public websites
3. Street signs
4. Residential and commercial realtors
5. Wholesalers

At first, you may not want or need access to all of them, but it's good to know a little about each for investments you will make today and in the future.

PRIVATE ONLINE DATABASE

There are several private, subscription-only online databases that offer access to properties listed for sale. In addition to property listings, they often provide valuation, historical sales details, property taxes paid, and leasing information to help buyers make better choices. The leading databases are Multiple Listing Service (MLS) for residential properties and rentals and COSTARS and LoopNet for commercial properties. While the cost for access to MLS is reasonable, COSTARS and LoopNet are expensive and thus are usually subscribed to by corporations doing sizable volumes of business.

PUBLIC ONLINE WEBSITES

For residential, single-family, and vacation homes, Realtor.com and Zillow .com are the most popular as of this writing. These sites are free to the public and can be used to research properties for sale or rent. As well, they can provide insights on historical home sales and values. The information provided for home values are not 100 percent accurate; however, they do provide you with a ballpark estimate you can use for analysis purposes. In addition to providing free access, these sites offer paid services that allow users to list properties for sale or rent. Public websites like these rarely list duplexes, triplexes, fourplexes, and commercial properties. So, if you're looking for multi-family or commercial properties, you're unlikely to find them here.

PROPERTY SIGNS

Despite the rise in electronic advertisement for properties for sale, the old school method of placing a sign outside the property is still nearly ubiquitous. The thinking behind it is that property signs are good at making locals aware of sales as well as attracting other folks already familiar with the area or neighborhood where the properties are for sale or rent.

LOCAL RESIDENTIAL AND COMMERCIAL REALTORS

Active, full-time realtors are always looking to sell real estate. The more active they are, the more knowledgeable they tend to be. If you see many signs and listings from a particular realtor, I recommend you start with them. If they're too busy to help you, they can refer you to others.

Realtors typically specialize in either commercial or residential properties. That's because there are more nuances to representing commercial properties than there are in residential real estate. Also, commercial realtors have a robust network of commercial property owners and purchasers to whom they often present deals, including an array of investors who they know can get the deal done quickly and efficiently. The brokers keep themselves attuned to what deals will hit the sweet spot of their investors and aim to sell a hot deal before it hits the streets.

If you don't have an established relationship with a commercial real estate broker, it may be difficult to get in early on a commercial deal. But don't let that dissuade you. I recommend you start building a relationship with at least two savvy commercial real estate brokers. Be prepared to prove to them that you have what it takes financially and experience-wise to close on a deal so that they'll work hard at presenting investment ideas to you.

WHOLESALERS

These are companies with a network of existing investors that call prospective sellers offering to sell their homes more quickly. They typically lock up the transaction by entering into a purchase agreement with the buyer, then flip the contract to investors. Wholesalers rarely close on the property itself, yet they make anywhere from 10–20 percent on the contract flip. In my experience, it's difficult to find a good deal when buying through a wholesaler, though I think it's worth looking into what deals they have available—in markets that you know well—to determine if a reasonable investment opportunity exists. Investors who do know the area, including its rents and housing values, strike quickly, so you must have a commensurate knowledge to beat them to the punch.

THE THREE ESSENTIAL CRITERIA WHEN CHOOSING WHICH PROPERTIES TO INVEST IN

Because you're starting from the bottom with limited financial resources, choosing properties that have serious potential to increase in value is essential. I use the following three criteria to determine if a property is worth further investigation.

1. LOCATION, LOCATION, LOCATION

I know that's only one criterion, but it's so important it deserves being repeated three times. Where you buy real estate has everything to do with the likelihood that it will appreciate. There are dozens of factors that go into determining value, such as price, convenience, the local school district, taxes—all of which depend upon location.

While we're on the topic of things that come in threes, I always ask myself three questions when trying to assess a property's location, all of which relate to its proximity to other places.

- **Is the property I'm interested in close to water (e.g., water-front, beachfront, walking distance to the beach, etc.)?**
  Proximity to water is an aesthetic consideration. People like to see water. They may never swim in it or even dip their toes

in, but they like to dine on the waterfront, walk or ride a bike around the water, and take it in as part of the landscape. Thus, proximity to water is its own form of equity.

- **Is it close enough to downtown that I can walk, take a quick Uber, or ride a few short train stops to get to the happening areas?** Downtown is about living close to employment opportunities, restaurants, events, and activities and about convenience. If you look at the downtown area in a major city like Chicago, you'll find that everything close to Lake Michigan and to downtown is consistently hot.

- **Is it close to public transportation?** Even if it's in the suburbs, is there well-maintained, accessible public transportation that makes it easy to get where all the action is? You might analyze a property and think, *Well, it's not near water, and it might be a bit further out from the city, but it's close to convenient transportation. A person can walk to that transportation and get into the city reasonably quickly.* To me, that property's still hot because being able to easily get to public transportation is the next best thing to living in the downtown area.

If the property satisfies all these criteria, then for me, that's either a hot property or soon to be one. In some cases, an area may not yet have been discovered; however, once folks realize its potential over time, the property values in the area will change accordingly. Notice how I said, "over time"? That's because it takes years for neighborhoods to transition (and consequently why it takes years to become a millionaire in real estate). Unless you have the capital to buy into neighborhoods that are already hot, you'll need to answer questions like these to discover the hidden potential for the future. The challenge is that without a crystal ball, you can never predict when the tide will shift. You won't be able to secure high rates for your rentals for some time. But if you stick to these criteria, investors will eventually see what you see, and you'll feel vindicated. I used this approach when I purchased my properties in Jersey City and Washington, DC, and it's paid out a hundred-fold. All these years later, I no longer have a difficult time finding tenants willing to pay me full market rents.

2. IS THE PROPERTY RENTING BELOW THE RENTAL MARKET RATE FOR THE AREA?

You must learn the specifics of the rental market where you are investing to gauge its potential and develop a strategy for increasing income, property valuation, and amplifying your net worth. This can take time, and sometimes, even after doing all the research, it takes the experience of jumping in to truly understand the market itself. What does a one-, two-, or three-bedroom property rent for? How much are the leases for retail stores or office buildings going for in your desired area? You'll find that properties in similar markets rent within a certain range of each other depending on the quality and amenities of the apartment building and space. Once you know what properties rent, lease, or even sell for, you can then determine if a property that you're looking to buy is undervalued, overvalued, or well-priced based on the rent roll. Using the combined rental information and operating cost, I'll show you how you can calculate other helpful metrics like the Cap Rate, cash-on-cash return, and price per door or per square foot to make your comparisons to other properties in the market and determine if you've found a diamond in the rough or just another rock.

3. IS THERE ANY UPSIDE POTENTIAL?

I always look for properties that have upside potential (additional land, community development plans, air rights, etc.) to generate more income. For example, if a property has enough land to add another house or building structure that can be rented out for additional income, you might want to consider it because you're in essence getting that land for a new property at no additional cost. Perhaps there are air rights you can use to expand your building or sell to a developer looking to build a high-rise building next door.

When I purchased my first three apartment buildings, the city had plans in the works to revitalize the neighborhoods, and the properties came with additional space to expand or build larger buildings. In one of the buildings, when the original owner and builder moved out, I added a wall on the third-floor apartment and converted three apartments and a retail store to four apartments and a retail store, thereby increasing my rents by $1,000 per month. The heaters in the property were not separately metered, so I was paying the heating bill for the post office plus the four units above it. Since they operated at different times, I was heating the building twenty-four hours a day, every day. I decided to invest $20,000 to install four new furnaces and individual apartment meters. This saved me thousands of dollars annually, and I quickly recouped my $20,000– investment.

The office building I purchased came with an additional commercial plot of land directly in front of the local commuter train. The road has an average of 17,500 vehicles passing daily. I plan on building ten salon studios on that land to earn an additional $120,000 a year in income. My cost will only be the cost of construction because the land came with my building and is being paid by the tenants of my office building.

Properties with upside potential are hidden gems, so keep a keen eye out for the potential of a property that the seller never realized. That's where valuation opportunities are born.

HOW TO ANALYZE AND EVALUATE A REAL ESTATE DEAL

The most common ways to determine the value of a real estate deal are the Comparable Sales Approach, the Construction Approach, and the Income Approach. These methods are largely dependent upon the type of real estate you are looking to purchase: single-family, commercial, or land. This is exactly the approach appraisers use to assess the value of commercial properties.

COMPARABLE SALES APPROACH

The Sales Comparison Approach seeks to identify properties of the same type, size, and condition to establish a comparable value. In other words, what are similar properties in the area selling for? Different price values are assigned to features, such as square footage, central air-conditioning, the number of bathrooms and half bathrooms, an attached garage, and so forth. Both Zillow.com and Realtor.com perform this same analysis using a sizable database of recent sales, similar in size, and within a certain radius of your property. Because these websites don't have insight into the quality of the property in question, such as new kitchens, updated flooring, and so forth, their estimated value is not 100 percent accurate, but it's close. This is the method most used for analyzing and evaluating the value of single-family homes. It's also used for commercial properties, though it's only one of many other data points used. COSTARS or Loop. Net maintain comparable sales for commercial properties, but you will need access to an account with these online services to find comparable commercial property sales.

CONSTRUCTION APPROACH

The construction approach evaluates the cost of erecting a building from scratch, rather than purchasing an existing structure(s). Investors look at the cost of land as well as the quantity and cost of materials and labor to be used in the building, which varies from market to market. They then assign a construction cost per square foot. That base cost gets multiplied by the size of the building to determine how much it would cost to rebuild or replace the entire property. For example, if the land costs $100,000, the building is 2,000 square feet, and the going rate for new construction is $300 per square foot, the cost assigned for a new building is $700,000 ($100,000 for the land and $600,000 to construct the building). If the existing building is being offered at $550,000 and buying it is therefore significantly cheaper than building a new one, this might be a worthwhile investment, assuming the condition and amenities of the existing building are favorable. This metric is commonly used to evaluate and analyze the value of commercial real estate, though I've used this approach to establish the value of a residential property as well. When you consider what it would cost to buy the land and build the same size house from scratch, you may realize that the asking price for an existing house is a good deal if the cost of purchasing it and improving it would still result in you paying less than you would to build the same size house on the same plot of land. Every deal is different.

INCOME APPROACH

The income approach looks at the income a property generates to determine the value of a property. This is the most common approach used to evaluate and analyze a commercial property. As you'll see in the following spreadsheet, I've provided an analysis of an actual two-unit property to show you how this approach works. The size of the property doesn't matter. All you need to do is include all the components of the rents and expenses to perform your analysis. Don't be intimidated by the seeming complexity of the spreadsheet; you'll get the hang of using it in no time.

To analyze a property, you must first know its total annual rental income, operating expenses (property taxes, maintenance, repairs, insurance, property management, etc.), and mortgage principal and interest. Landlords looking to sell their properties will have records, tax returns, and/or financial reports showing the monthly and annual money they're taking in from rental income as well as the expenses they're paying out. The most critical financial reports are the rent roll, net income statements, and balance sheet statements for the past three to five years. This information is vital to your analysis.

Before continuing, let's take a closer look at some key terms that will make this approach more understandable.

- **Net Operating Income, or NOI**, is the total amount of rent income you expect to receive on a property in a year, minus the operating expenses to keep it running (including any income lost due to vacancies). Operating expenses include property taxes, maintenance, repairs, insurance, property management, and so forth. Mortgage principal and mortgage interest are not included in determining a property's NOI.
- **Cash-on-cash or return on investment (ROI)** measures what percentage of the funds you've invested that you're receiving back as profit. The profit on a deal is your total rental income

minus operating expenses, mortgage interest, and principal. The cash investment is the down payment, closing costs, appraisal costs, and any costs associated with inspecting or acquiring the property. To determine ROI, divide the annual cash profit you expect to receive by the amount you invested. Say you expected to receive $700 in yearly income from a $10,000–investment, your ROI would be .07 percent or 7 percent per year. This is how you compare one deal to another to determine which one is financially best for you.

- **Capitalization rate commonly known as Cap Rate is a ratio**, equal to annual net operating income divided by purchase price (annual NOI/purchase price). The higher the Cap Rate, the greater the ROI, and therefore, the more valuable the property. Cap Rate assumes that you're paying all cash for the property, and it allows you to compare similar or dissimilar investments (e.g., apartment house versus a restaurant investment) on an equal playing field. So, if one property investment offered a Cap Rate of 7 percent while a restaurant or commercial real estate investment offered a Cap Rate of 10 percent (on the same amount of invested capital for both deals), you can quickly see that the 10 percent deal is more financially favorable.

- **Price per square foot** is calculated by taking the total price and dividing it by the total square footage. For example, a $1 million–property that contained 10,000 square feet would have a price per square foot of $100. Price per square foot is an excellent metric to ensure that you're paying close to or less than the going price of similar-sized real estate.

- **Price per door**, such as with multiple units in an apartment building, is calculated by taking the total price and dividing it by the total number of entry doors or individual units. For example, a ten-unit apartment building being offered for $1 million has a price per door of $100,000. A fifteen-unit apartment building around the corner being offered at $1,200,000 has a price per door of $80,000. On the surface, the fifteen-unit building appears to be the better deal because you'd pay $20,000 less per door. But price per door is only one measure of a deal's value. You'd also have to look at the property's condition, the deferred maintenance, the number of one, two, and three bedrooms in each building, as well as the amenities each building offers to determine which is the better deal.

Below is an example of how I analyze multi-family properties to make a buy or no-buy decision on purchasing a property. You can download this template for free on my website at www.cedricnash.com.

Multi-Family Property Acquisition Analysis

Deal Section		Rent Roll Section		
Asking Price	$359,900.00	Unit #	Description	Current Rent
Discount	($0.00)	1	1 Bedroom, 1 Bath	$1,400.00
Sale Price	**$359,900.00**	2	1 Bedroom, 1 Bath	$1,600.00
Dn Payment (10%)	($35,990.00)			
Mortgage	$323,910.00			**$3,000.00**
Term in Years	30			
Interest Rate	4.00%			
Discount Rate on Asking Price	0.00%			
Est. Closing Costs (2% of Sales Price)	$7,198.00			

Revenue Section					
Rent Increase		4%	4%	4%	4%
Description of Account	**Year 1**	**Year 2**	**Year 3**	**Year 4**	**Year 5**
Income 5100					
Rental Income	$ 3,000	$ 3,120	$ 3,245	$ 3,375	$ 3,510
Total Rent Income at 100%	**$ 3,000**	**$ 3,120**	**$ 3,245**	**$ 3,375**	**$ 3,510**
Vacancies 5200					
Apartments (5%)	$ 150	$ 156	$ 162	$ 169	$ 175
Total Vacancies	**$ 150**	**$ 156**	**$ 162**	**$ 169**	**$ 175**
Net Rental Income	**$ 2,850**	**$ 2,964**	**$ 3,083**	**$ 3,206**	**$ 3,334**
Other Revenue 5800					
Laundry & Vending	$ -	$ -	$ -	$ -	$ -
Late Charges	$ -	$ -	$ -	$ -	$ -
Total Other Revenue	**$ -**	**$ -**	**$ -**	**$ -**	**$ -**
Total Revenue	**$ 2,850**	**$ 2,964**	**$ 3,083**	**$ 3,206**	**$ 3,334**

Operating Expenses Section					
Utilities 6400					
Fuel Oil	$ -	$ -	$ -	$ -	$ -
Gas	$ -	$ -	$ -	$ -	$ -
Electricity	$ -	$ -	$ -	$ -	$ -
Water/Sewer	$ 71	$ 71	$ 71	$ 71	$ 71
Total Utility Expense	**$ 71**	**$ 71**	**$ 71**	**$ 71**	**$ 71**
Maintenance Expense 6500					
Janitor/Cleaning Supplies	$ -	$ -	$ -	$ -	$ -
Janitor/Cleaning Contract	$ -	$ -	$ -	$ -	$ -
Exterminating Contract	$ -	$ -	$ -	$ -	$ -
Exterminating Supplies	$ -	$ -	$ -	$ -	$ -
Garbage/Trash Removal	$ -	$ -	$ -	$ -	$ -
Landscaping Supplies	$ -	$ -	$ -	$ -	$ -
Landscaping Contract	$ -	$ -	$ -	$ -	$ -
Repair Supplies	$ -	$ -	$ -	$ -	$ -
Repair Contract	$ -	$ -	$ -	$ -	$ -
Elevator Maint./Contract	$ -	$ -	$ -	$ -	$ -
Heating/Cooling Repairs/Maint.	$ -	$ -	$ -	$ -	$ -
Snow Removal	$ -	$ -	$ -	$ -	$ -
Total Maintenance Expense	**$ 285**	**$ 296**	**$ 308**	**$ 321**	**$ 333**

Multi-Family Property Acquisition Analysis
continued

Description of Account	Year 1	Year 2	Year 3	Year 4	Year 5
Taxes & Insurance 6700					
Real Estate Taxes	$ 600	$ 600	$ 600	$ 600	$ 600
Misc. Taxes/Licenses/Permits	$ -	$ -	$ -	$ -	$ -
Prop. & Liability Ins. (Hazard)	$ 300	$ 300	$ 300	$ 300	$ 300
Total Taxes & Insurance	**$ 900**	**$ 900**	**$ 900**	**$900**	**$900**
Total Operating Expenses	**$ 1,256**	**1,267**	**$1,279**	**$1,291**	**$1,304**
Net Operating Income	**$ 1,594**	**1,697**	**1,803**	**1,914**	**2,030**
Finance Section					
Financial Expense 6800					
Int. on Bonds Payable		$ -	$ -	$ -	$ -
Int. on Mortgage Payable	$ 1,080	$ 1,080	$ 1,080	$ 1,080	$ 1,080
Int. on Notes Payable (Long Term)		$ -	$ -	$ -	$ -
Int. on Notes Payable (Short Term)		$ -	$ -	$ -	$ -
Mortgage Insurance Premiums		$ -	$ -	$ -	$ -
Misc. Financial Expenses		$ -	$ -	$ -	$ -
Replacement Reserve Withdrawals		$ -	$ -	$ -	$ -
Capital Expenditures		$ -	$ -	$ -	$ -
Principal Payments	$ 467	$ 467	$ 467	$ 467	$ 467
Debt Service (Section 241 Loan)		$ -	$ -	$ -	$ -
Debt Service Reserve (Section 202)		$ -	$ -	$ -	$ -
General Operating Reserve		$ -	$ -	$ -	$ -
Total Financial Expense	**$ 1,546**	**1,546**	**1,546**	**1,546**	**1,546**
Analysis Section					
Monthly Total Cost of Operations	**$ 2,802**	**2,814**	**2,825**	**2,838**	**2,851**
Monthly Total Revenue	**$ 2,850**	**2,964**	**3,083**	**3,206**	**3,334**
Monthly Profit/Loss (Cash Flow)	**$ 48**	**150**	**257**	**368**	**483**
Annual Profit/Loss (Cash Flow)	**$ 573**	**1,804**	**3,085**	**4,417**	**5,801**
Annual Leveraged Cash-on - Cash Return on Investment (ROI)	1.99%	6.27%	10.71%	15.34%	20.15%
Average Price Per Door	$179,950				
Current Capitalization Rate (Assumes I'm Paying Cash for the Property)	5.3%	5.66%	6.01%	6.38%	6.77%
Annual Income Earned at the Current Cap Rate	$19,075				
The Property's Value at a 7% Cap Rate (Based on the NOI Earned on the Property)	$273,286	$290,874	$309,166	$328,190	$347,975
Monthly Cash-on-Cash Return I Would Earn if I Purchased the Property at a 7% Cap Rate	$2,099				
Annual Cash-on-Cash Return I Would Earn if I Purchased the Property at a 7% Cap Rate	$25,193				

Each of the main evaluation sections are highlighted in red: Deal, Rent Roll, Revenue, Operating Expenses, Net Operating Expenses, Finance, and Analysis. This spreadsheet contains monthly expense numbers unless specified otherwise in the left-hand description column. I usually add additional columns of similar information to do "what if" analyses based on a variety of assumptions, such as asking price, rental increases, etc. This provides me with all the financial information I need to make quick decisions while negotiating a deal.

The Deal Section

This is an overview of the deal that specifies price as well as any discounts on the asking price I might offer, depending on the market. Here I also specify the down payment required, the amount I'll be financing, the mortgage terms in years, the interest rate, and the estimated closing costs. For larger deals, I add additional columns to compare the different deal scenarios and evaluate the property's full potential.

Rent Roll Section

Here's where you'll see the current rents received per unit, the number of bedrooms per unit, and the total rents being received by the property. Usually, property owners provide you with a rent roll of current tenants. You need to verify that the information is accurate by making sure that the rental income aligns with the rent roll and that there are current leases for the amounts provided on the rent roll. If any units are vacant, then I jot down $0 in rent, so I can get an accurate account of what I'm dealing with.

You should perform your own analysis of the rents by looking at apartments for rent in the nearby area (using Zillow.com or Rent.com) and determine if the current rents are too low, too high, or about where they should be. If the existing rents look comparatively low, that's the sign of a potentially good deal. It means you've got an upside opportunity to increase rental revenue and thus net income. If the rents are on the high side, then you may need to determine if you could potentially lose tenants to other properties in the surrounding area.

For larger deals, I create additional columns to model rental increases over the next five years and thereby evaluate how the property will perform over a five-year period. That's because, in the first year, the deal may not be financially attractive; though by year three or four, it could turn out to be a great deal. I want to consider and evaluate how the property will perform over time as part of my decision-making process.

Revenue Section

In this section, I document the total monthly rents minus a vacancy factor, plus any additional income that the property offers. For example, late fees and laundry services are considered additional income. In this example, I used a vacancy factor of 5 percent, slightly below the industry standard of 7 percent. The vacancy factor is the percentage of the rent that you won't collect due to units being temporarily vacant, tenant turnover, or prolonged vacancy periods.

For larger, high-priced properties, I use a vacancy factor of 10 percent because I prefer to be more conservative in my analysis. If the deal still works with a 10 percent vacancy factor, then I can feel even more comfortable, though I'll still strive to achieve 5 percent vacancy to create more revenue and income in the end. Large commercial property vacancies can run for long periods of time, so as an investor, you must make sure you either have other income streams to rely upon or the cash reserves to endure prolonged vacancies until your marketing efforts land you the perfect tenant.

Operating Expenses Section

In this section, I document all the expenses to operate the property, including utilities, maintenance, taxes, and insurance. The previous building owner usually provides this information. They should have clear, concise, and accurate accounting records. You can use their costs as a starting point, though there are exceptions. For example, because you're likely to pay more for the property than the previous owner, the cost of your insurance and property taxes will tend to be higher than the current owner's. You can quickly and easily get a quote for insurance and add 2 percent of the purchase price as a placeholder for what you can expect to pay in annual property taxes until you get a more accurate number from the local tax assessor's office.

The sum of all your expenses is called the Total Operating Expenses.

Net Operating Income (NOI)

NOI, as explained previously, equals the Net Rental Income minus the Total Operating Expenses. NOI is essential for determining a property's capitalization rate (Cap Rate). Commercial realtors commonly refer to a property's NOI, so if you plan on upping your game, you'll need to get comfortable understanding NOI.

Finance Section

How much will you pay in monthly loan principal and interest? To calculate your anticipated mortgage payments, use the assumptions provided in the Deal Section, such as your loan amount (which is the asking price minus your down payment), interest rate, and loan terms (number of years you plan on financing the property, typically thirty years for residential and twenty-five years for commercial) to calculate your loan interest and principal amounts. You can plug these assumptions into the mortgage formula provided by Excel or by using a mortgage calculator to calculate your mortgage payment amount (available at www.cedricnash.com). Once you know the mortgage interest payment and principal payment, you can plug them into your spreadsheet.

Analysis Section

In this section, the final numbers are prepared to comprehensively analyze the deal. I calculate these eleven factors:

1. Monthly total cost of operations (monthly net operating income plus interest and principal payment)
2. Monthly total revenue (total monthly rents minus vacancy factor plus other income from late fees, laundry, etc.)
3. Monthly profit/loss cash flow (monthly total revenue minus monthly total cost of operations)
4. Annual profit/loss cash flow (monthly profit/loss cash flow times twelve months)
5. Annual leveraged cash-on-cash return on investment (annual profit and loss divided by the sum of down payment plus the closing costs)
6. Average price per door (sales price divided by the two apartments)
7. Current capitalization (Cap Rate) (monthly net operating income times twelve months divided by the sales price), which assumes that I am paying cash for the property
8. Annual income earned at the current Cap Rate (sales price times the current Cap Rate of 5.32 percent)

9. The property's value at a 7 percent Cap Rate based on the current NOI earned on the property (monthly NOI times twelve months divided by 7 percent Cap Rate)

10. Monthly cash-on-cash return I would earn if I had purchased the property at a 7 percent Cap Rate (sales price times 7 percent divided by twelve)

11. Annual cash-on-cash return I would earn if I purchased the property at a 7 percent Cap Rate (sales price times 7 percent Cap Rate).

BUY OR NO-BUY DECISION POINTS

As you can see in the analysis section of the previous spreadsheet, in Year 1, the property is only offering a 1.99 percent cash-on-cash return on investment with a Cap Rate of 5.3 percent. After investing approximately $43,188 in cash, which includes the down payment and closing costs, an investor would receive a 1.99 percent return, which translates to $48 in monthly cash flow profit or $573 in annual cash flow profit. If an investor paid off 100 percent of the property in cash (i.e., no mortgage) at a 5.3 percent Cap Rate, they would earn $1,594.16 per month ($359,900 × 5.3% divided by 12 months), or $19,074.70 annually ($359,900 × 5.3%). Using the net operating income that the property is generating, and assuming a Cap Rate of 7 percent, the value of the property is $272,495.71 (monthly NOI of $1,594.16 × 12 months divided by 7% Cap Rate).

I would look at this deal cautiously because at my ideal return on investment level of 7 percent, the property listing appears to be overpriced (list price of $359,900 versus $273,286 at a 7 percent cash-on-cash return on investment). The average price per door is $179,000 ($359,900 divided by two apartments). Given the current sales price, the high market demand for investment properties, and the seller's unwillingness to lower the sales price, I would need to net $2,099 monthly ($359,900 × 7% ROI divided by 12 months) or $25,193 annually ($359,900 × 7% ROI) from the property to realize my ideal 7 percent return on investment.

Cap Rate is a powerful tool, which is why most commercial realtors and lenders commonly discuss property and income values in terms of it. Cap Rate allows you to compare not only two different deals but two different types of deals equally, even investments as different from each other as an apartment and a retail restaurant property.

My goal is always to receive a minimum of 5 percent and ideally a compounding 7 percent or higher annual cash-on-cash return on my investments so that I can double my money every ten years. I like 7 percent because there are always expenses that I neglect to account for, so 7 percent gives me enough cushion to make the deal worthwhile. As of this writing, banks are paying less than 1 percent interest on money in a savings account. With inflation averaging 6.2 percent, money sitting in the bank depreciates rapidly. The example deal we analyzed with a 5.3 percent Cap Rate was reasonable; however, at a 1.99 percent cash-on-cash return, it was not a worthwhile use of my capital, and therefore, I passed on purchasing it. The property did have some upside potential, but given record levels of inflation in 2021 and the uncertainty of future real estate values and rents, I decided to search for something more favorable. Your goals may be different, though now that you understand how to calculate a property's cash-on-cash return, Cap Rate, and average price per door, you can establish thresholds for your own opportunities and search out the right investments accordingly.

TAX BENEFITS OF INVESTING IN REAL ESTATE

As we discussed previously, the US tax code is extremely favorable to the real estate industry, and to you as a real estate investor. Here are two of the main reasons why:

DEPRECIATED INCOME

Real Estate investment assets (residential investment and commercial properties only, not land) are depreciated over a twenty-seven-and-a-half-year period. That means that every year the value of the building goes down *on paper*, and that amount is spread across twenty-seven and a half years. This lowers the net rental income you must claim on your tax returns every year, even though the amount you keep is not necessarily going down.

So, let's say you purchased a property for $300,000. You would depreciate that property on your tax return by $10,909 per year for twenty-seven and a half years. Even if you received, say, $21,000 a year in net income after expenses, you would still only be taxed on $10,091 ($21,000 minus $10,909). The depreciation amount stays the same. When you eventually sell the property, you will be required to recapture the depreciation (which effectively increases your proceeds at the time of the sale and thus your tax bill), but you'll still benefit from many if not all those years of depreciated income.

1031 EXCHANGES

The 1031 provision in the IRS Code allows you to exchange one investment property for another without having to pay capital gains taxes on your profit, so long as a qualified intermediary (e1031xChange, to name one) guides the process and ensures the exchange happens as it is supposed to.

Whenever you sell a property and make a profit (and I hope you will many times), it creates a taxable capital gain. For example, if you invest $10,000 to purchase a property and your net proceeds after you sell the property are $100,000, you have a $90,000 capital gain (plus recaptured depreciation). Ordinarily, you'd have to pay capital gains taxes to the IRS on the $90,000, plus the recaptured depreciation you benefited from for the past twenty-seven or so years of owning the property.

With a 1031 exchange, your 1031 receiver will receive the $90,000– proceeds after your sale. This way, instead of paying the capital gains tax and recaptured depreciation to the IRS now, you'll continue to have all that money available to grow your real estate portfolio. You can make a heftier down payment and purchase a larger new property than you would otherwise be able to without the 1031 exchange. Ideally, by investing in a larger property, you will yield more income, higher appreciation, and greater wealth.

The following are the 6 rules that must be adhered to for a successful 1031 exchange:

1. You must purchase another "like-kind" *investment* property.
2. The replacement property must be of equal or greater value.
3. You must invest all the proceeds from the sale.
4. The titleholder and taxpayer must be the same as previously.
5. The property must be identified within forty-five days.
6. The new property must be purchased within 180 days of the sale.

Only you or your financial adviser can determine the rate of return that best suits your financial goals. Yet, armed with the ability to find and properly analyze real estate deals, it's only a matter of time before you too begin to put the "real" into real estate.

HOW TO MANAGE THE RISKS ASSOCIATED WITH
INVESTING IN REAL ESTATE

The secret to managing the risks of real estate investing is to own several properties in varied locations across all real estate types: residential, commercial, retail, office, land, and industrial. As was the case with securities investments, diversification is central to risk mitigation. Too much of one type of real estate in one area can hurt you financially if there is a downturn in demand. A recent example is the COVID-19 pandemic, which created serious problems for multiple, commercial, office space owners because so many retail businesses failed and other businesses sought to minimize the demand for office space by allowing employees to work remotely.

If you're adequately diversified, you'll always have a hedge against major losses until things turn back to normal or until you're able to develop another in-demand use for your property.

PROFESSIONAL PROPERTY MANAGEMENT
VERSUS SELF MANAGEMENT

Many folks shy away from investing in real estate because they don't want to be a landlord. The truth is they don't have to be. They can always hire a professional property manager to do it for them, though what's even truer is this: you can successfully manage the property yourself and save some money through consistent dedication, focus, and effort. You might even end up liking the job.

Professional property managers provide services based upon your needs. Their services range from leasing, move-ins, rent collection, bookkeeping, construction, maintenance, repairs, move-outs, unit turnarounds, and evictions. Property managers typically charge from 3–15 percent of the monthly rental income, depending on the number of units within the property. The larger the number of units, the lower percentage their fee will be. Property management on a single-family or vacation rental home tends to range in the double digits. They take their fees directly from the rents received. It's a significant amount of money; money which could be going into your pocket or your Freedom Fund instead. However, if you don't have the time to consistently tend to your property management duties, you may have no choice but to hire your own property manager.

If you do elect to hire a professional property management company, make sure to find them via referral, so you know they have a good track record. Review your property management contract, and be sure the services that you need are well documented and can be provided. I recommend you sign a six-month contract initially, which can be terminated with thirty days' notice, and assess how they perform before renewing it. In your agreement, make sure that the property management company provides three bids for all repair and maintenance work to be performed on your property. Is it clear if they're receiving a construction management fee for coordinating maintenance and repairs? Some professional property managers provide maintenance and repair services at cost while others charge a fee for coordinating and managing maintenance and repair work. Know the fees associated with any evictions. Will legal services be needed or not? In some states, property managers can evict tenants without the use of a lawyer; while in other states, if the owner of the property is a corporation or an LLC, they must have a lawyer represent the entity. In short, make sure you know exactly what you are getting and not getting for the fee they're charging. You want them to be solving your problems, not creating new ones.

I've been managing my own properties in-house for decades, and I've always known how important owning a portfolio of real estate was to my wealth journey. I saw several of my mentors sitting pretty by owning hundreds of apartment units, so I changed my mindset to embrace the challenge of property management instead of shying away from it. The main goal of successful property management is to keep your tenants living peacefully in your space(s), paying their rent on time, and accepting annual rent increases. As I've shown you above in the explanation of cash-on-cash return and Cap Rate, the value of your properties is linked to stable rising rents because investors are buying the income stream your properties produce. So, keeping good paying tenants in your properties is key. That's part of why my property management philosophy is based on two guiding principles that allow me to achieve my goals:

1. Be fair but be firm.
2. Respond fast to get more.

Fair and firm is the kind of relationship you need to have with your tenants. Fair in all your dealings and always respectful in your treatment of your tenants. Remember, they're your customer, and you want that customer to continue living in your property and paying on time. However, there can sometimes be a blurry line between business and friendship, and that's a prescription for trouble. Keep that line clearly delineated, so all parties can see it. Be friendly of course, but be careful about becoming too chummy. You must maintain a position where you can leave the business relationship when you need to without creating collateral damage. For instance, I stay out of my tenants' personal and financial affairs and the, ahem, stories that go along with them. My payment requirements are fair and automatic, without any emotional baggage attached. Truth is, I am genuinely sorry when my tenants run into financial hardship, but my lender is not, and they'll take my property from me if I fail to pay them on time. So, when tenants fail to pay me on time, I start the eviction process immediately in hopes that they will make good before we must resolve the matter in court. I'm saying this because this is a common area where tenant friendships get murky to the financial detriment of landlords. Landlords who don't have the time or inclination to replace non-paying tenants or go to court often close their eyes and cross their fingers hoping the tenant comes up with the money to pay their rent. Before too long the tenant realizes that the owner won't go through with an eviction, so they continue to pay late and hold the landlord hostage. This isn't everyone, though you can be sure of this: it is, or will be, someone you rent to. You must always manage the relationship at a level that allows you to successfully perform your primary role as a property owner and manager first; otherwise, both of you end up out of the property.

When things break or wear out, as they are bound to do; your job is to respond quickly and thoroughly. Do your job correctly, and when it's time for rent increases, your tenants won't hassle you. When a tenant calls for service, which is not that often if you stay on top of your properties, it's critical that you respond quickly. If you start avoiding unpleasant situations, hoping that they will somehow go away, you'll only make things worse and cause yourself and your tenants more frustration. So, you must do whatever it takes, even if it means taking vacation time off work or tending to the issue(s) before or after work or on weekends. You need to demonstrate to your tenants that you care and are responsive. If you do so, your tenants are far more likely to stay in your unit, continue to pay on time, accept rent increases without complaining, and thereby contribute to your success as an investor.

Here are a few tips that will help you manage your own properties profitably, thereby accelerating your journey to Destination Millionaire and beyond.

GRIND TO KEEP YOUR PROPERTIES FULLY OCCUPIED

Given the combined demands of job and family, it's difficult to find time to do it all as a landlord, but vacancies cost you and your family money. You simply must do whatever it takes to increase your odds of landing a tenant, and a good one at that. It's easy to shy away from this responsibility, and it's one of the main reasons why people don't want to be landlords. If you choose to be a landlord, embrace the task of leasing up your properties. Once you become an expert at it, you will forever be empowered and won't need to be troubled when a tenant elects to move out or needs to be evicted. You're on the road to Destination Millionaire, so it's time to change your mindset and embrace the opportunity to master leasing as a personal challenge.

START ALL TENANT EVALUATIONS WITH A RENTAL APPLICATION

Know who you are renting to. For the safety of the people living in your building, and to ensure that the person is who they say they are, make it mandatory for every potential tenant to complete a rental application and provide a government-issued photo ID. In the rental application, you will ask for their:

- Name
- Address
- Social security number
- Employment history

- Salary information
- Employer verification contact
- Rental history
- Rental verification contact
- Rental references
- Co-signer section with all the co-signers' social security information
- Signature and date section

In the signature and date section, make sure you include a statement whereby the prospective tenant acknowledges that, by signing the application, they are authorizing you to contact their employer to verify their employment and income and run a credit and background check on them. Performing an employment and rental reference check will give you a sense of the tenant's ability to pay their rent and how reliably they've paid their rent and conducted themselves at their previous places of residence. To ensure that they can reasonably afford to rent your space, be careful that the rent you're charging doesn't exceed 30 percent of the tenant's gross monthly income. (For a $1,000/month apartment, the tenant should make at least $1,000/30 percent, which equals $3,333.33 per month in gross income, or $40,000 per year.) The credit check will give you a sense of how consistent they are about paying their bills. The social security number ensures you're talking to the right person. I've had situations where tenant names were identical to a registered sex offender's. I had to go the extra mile to verify the actual identity of my prospective tenant. The background check allows you to determine if your tenant has a pending or past criminal history that could put you or your tenants in danger. While you don't want to discriminate against tenants for their past conduct, when you spot a pattern, you need to believe it and take it strongly into consideration.

All the application information obtained prepares you in case you must perform an eviction. Not everyone turns out to be the person they claim to be, and in legal proceedings especially, accuracy matters.

NEVER MOVE A TENANT IN WITHOUT A SIGNED LEASE

Seems obvious, right? You'd be surprised at how many self-managed property landlords allow tenants to move in with the hope or promise of getting a signed lease later. This often happens because part-time landlords are busy with their regular jobs and being a landlord is only their side hustle. But when you think about it, there are agreed-upon rules at your main hustle as well as your side hustle. Otherwise, you don't get to go to work. Make that a rule at your properties as well. No keys without a signed lease, and take photos or video of the property at the time of move in. Was that door broken when you handed over the property? What about that hole in the wall behind it? Why argue about it at move-out time? Honestly, why create the chance for arguments at all?

To find a lease, look online for sample lease templates. Research and review your local applicable landlord/tenant laws, and be sure that your lease complies with them. For example, some local laws require rents to be paid by the fourth of the month, while others require rent to be paid by the fifth day of the month before they are considered late. It's essential that your lease complies with all local laws so that, if you end up in court, your case won't be dismissed outright because of an illegal lease.

GET YOUR RENTAL INCREASES

One of the primary wealth-building benefits of owning properties is the right to raise rents 3–5 percent annually, which allows us to stay ahead of inflation and earn income to be reinvested elsewhere. It is imperative that you secure those rent increases, or you will begin to lose money rather than build wealth. Insurance costs, property taxes, and maintenance costs increase. Commercial loans adjust every five years, so if interest rates are rising, then your mortgage payments will rise too. If you don't get rent increases, your net cash flow will quickly erode.

Another long-term factor to keep in mind is that, if you allow your rents to fall behind market rates now, the value of your property will diminish when you eventually sell your property. Remember, multi-family and commercial properties are valued based on the net cash flow of the property. If your net cash flow is low because your rents are way below market, then you will have a more difficult time justifying a higher offering price for your property. So-called "shark investors" look for opportunities where landlords are unaware of the market value of their rents. The sharks see that they can increase their cash flow immediately, simply, by legally increasing the rents to market rate because the existing owner failed to do so.

Make sure you have a clause in your leases stating that rents will be increased annually at 3–5 percent, depending on market conditions. Send your tenants a letter a couple months before the increases are set to go into effect, so they have ample notice. If they protest along the lines of "I've been such a good tenant," then use your discretion. Maybe they have been excellent tenants; if so, perhaps you can accept 3 percent or 4 percent instead of 5 percent. Good tenants are not only pleasant; they save you money and headaches on repairs they do themselves, as well as fixtures they take good care of. It's good policy to build friendly relationships with your tenants, so long as you always operate your business as a for-profit business and not as a friendship or charity.

RESPOND TO TENANT CALLS FOR REPAIRS QUICKLY

As a landlord, you must keep a cash reserve for building repairs and maintenance. I recommend 10 percent of your rental income so that you have sufficient cash to make building repairs. I've learned over time that dealing with tenant issues is easy if you take the correct perspective quickly. You must put yourself in their shoes. If you're living in a place with issues, such as a leak, a broken toilet, or a lack of hot water, you want to call someone and have them respond quickly, not hassle you. When a tenant has an issue, I get right on it. I fix it as quickly as I can to make the stress go away for both of us. Yes, it may cost me a little money to make them happy, but a happy tenant is a paying tenant. It makes your life so much easier and stress-free when your tenant is not complaining. Often, they complain about something that will improve your own property in the long run. I'll say that again for emphasis. *They're often complaining about something that will improve your investment property, so you win in the long run.* Therefore, don't panic or stress out. Fix the problem right away, and think of it as improving your investment. When it's time for that annual rent increase, you can approach them even more confidently, knowing that you responded to their needs.

There are some cases where tenants will never be happy. You'll respond to their every request but to no avail. That's why you need to know when to hold 'em and when to fold 'em. If you end up with a tenant that you can't ever make happy, the best approach is to depart ways as quickly as possible. You will be momentarily short on rent, but that's what your vacancy budget is for. That 5–10 percent you put away will help you ride out the storm until you find a better tenant for your unit.

LOOK FOR WAYS TO INCREASE THE VALUE OF YOUR PROPERTIES

Styles change over time, and since you compete for tenants, you need to continue investing in upgrades to your properties. Is it time to remodel your kitchens and bathrooms? Do your common areas need updating? Could you decrease your monthly NOI by installing separate heating and cooling systems in each unit so that tenants can pay for their own utilities individually rather than you paying for everyone's heat and air conditioning? Lower NOI means higher net profit and higher value at sale time; that's how that money spent is not only recouped but profitable to your bottom line.

As a skilled property manager, you should be asking yourself all sorts of questions like these regularly, and if the answer is yes, get right on it. The longer you wait, the less likely you'll be to attract the most reliable and affluent tenants among the existing tenant pool for your property type.

INSPECT YOUR UNITS MONTHLY

Properties wear over time, and tenants create excess damage. The only way to know what's going on in the units of your properties is to inspect them consistently. I recommend that you do a thorough walk-through of each of your units once a month. Create a checklist of items to inspect and walk around with a clipboard looking for and documenting leaking toilets and faucets, ceiling damage from a possible leaking roof, or damage to appliances, doors, windows, and flooring. Immediately remedy items on your checklist to minimize costs in the long run. Non-standard wear and tear to your property should not be tolerated, and you may be required to evict a tenant based on how they treat your property. A running toilet or leaking faucet can cost you up to $300 per month per fixture in wasted water bills. That's literally pouring money down the drain. It's imperative to keep an eye on your property regularly to save money and time in the long run. It also sends a message to your tenant that you're watching how they treat your property.

MANAGING EVICTIONS FIRMLY AND QUICKLY

The worst part of property management is having to deal with tenants who fail to pay or whose residency is making it unpleasant for the rest of your tenants. In some cases, being a good guy and doing the right thing is still not enough. You may feel you've done everything possible not to have to take a tenant to court. But you need to pay your creditors and stop losing money on unpaid rent. Evictions cost money if you must involve an attorney, and they take valuable time away from your other money-making or recreational activities. The reality is evictions are inevitable. Here's the best way to handle them.

Step one in the eviction process is to begin it on the first day the tenant's rent is late. You need to send them an email, certified letter, text message, and voice-mail message informing them that their rent is late and that you are starting the eviction process. Inform them that if you receive a payment within two days of the notification's date, then the eviction process will cease, and no eviction processing fee will be charged. Only the late fee outlined in their signed lease will be charged until it is paid. Your tenant needs to know that you will be reporting the late rent to the credit agencies. This may help inspire them to pay you if they value their credit scores. (Typically, their scores won't be affected unless they're late by more than thirty days.)

Step two is to file the eviction paperwork immediately. If you are operating as an LLC or corporation, some states will require that you have an attorney file the eviction and appear in court on behalf of the LLC or corporation. The court will mail you a court date. It is imperative that you or your attorney show up and present your case. If the tenant fails to appear or reschedules, then the court will likely award you a judgment and possession of your property, and you will be able to schedule with the sheriff's department to have the tenant's belongings removed and the locks changed. Hopefully, things never get to this point.

If the tenant does appear in court at the appointed time, the judge will hear their case. If it's deemed that they have a justifiable reason to withhold rent, then the judge may force you to resolve the issues and come back to court to ensure that you've done so. In most states, there is no legal reason to withhold rent. Maintenance and repair issues are not a legal reason to withhold rent, for example; however, judges usually force landlords to resolve any reasonable issues the tenant may have and allow time for them to pay any delinquent rent.

If the tenant is simply having financial issues, the judge typically forces the tenant and landlord to enter into a payment agreement allowing the tenant time to catch up. Judges generally prefer not to force tenants out of their homes, so they will give them time to make good on their commitment. The judge will set another court date so that they can verify that the tenant is adhering to the agreement. This could take up to thirty days before you reappear in court. By then, if the tenant has paid up all delinquent rent and late fees, the case will be dropped, and the tenant will be able to remain in the property. This could go on several times before the judge allows you to evict a tenant for continually paying late and having to reappear in court.

The whole process may take 60–120 days before the tenant is removed. In some states, it can even take years. Your only recourse is the security deposit that you received when the tenant moved in. Evictions are never fun, and you will lose a little money no matter what. The point is to be efficient and not waste time getting the process started. You can't afford to drag it out. However, despite the cost, the stress, and the frustration, you will not often run into a nightmare eviction. That's why owning rental property is still supremely worth it. Eviction is a risk, something you know by now comes with any sort of investment. That risk can be mitigated by setting firm, reasonable rules in your leases and insisting that both parties adhere to them. If you step up to the plate and put forth the effort, you will learn much, save a great deal, and ultimately succeed as a property manager.

HOW TO BECOME A MILLIONAIRE INVESTING IN REAL ESTATE

Here's a progression of best practices with which to pave your road to millionaire-level wealth and beyond, through real estate investing starting from the bottom:

1. Determine how much investment capital you can save from each paycheck, based on how much more you're earning by paying and consuming less.

2. Once you've grown your Freedom Fund to Level 3 of the M$M investment ladder ($25,000–$50,000), your credit score is 650 or higher, your income-to-debt ratio meets your lender's borrowing requirements, and you find yourself in a buyer's market (seven months or more of housing inventory supply), it's time to jump in and invest in a single-family or duplex, triplex, or fourplex. If it's a seller's market and the numbers don't yet meet your threshold, keep saving. Your additional savings still adds to your wealth journey towards Destination Millionaire.

3. Depending upon which strategy you've chosen (buy-and-hold or flip), hold your first property for three to five years, or flip that property when it's ready; then, invest in a small, multi-family property or a larger multi-family, commercial, or mixed-use property. Continue to earn and save as your property income piles up, then purchase additional properties. Take advantage of the 1031 exchange rules to save on taxes and transfer the maximum amount of your sales proceeds into your next, larger investment.

4. Hold your multi-family or commercial property for three to seven years; sell it and purchase an even larger apartment building, mixed-use, or commercial property.

5. As you earn more income from your main hustle, side hustle, securities investments, and real estate, consistently invest more capital into real estate until you achieve your desired endgame. Otherwise, once you accumulate enough capital, invest in entrepreneurship or alternative investments (angel, VC, hedge funds, private equity), which we'll cover in the next supplemental chapter.

6. As you approach your endgame, transition your real estate portfolio to high-quality triple net leased (NNN) properties where you can earn 5 percent-plus without lifting a finger to maintain your property. By this point, your capital should be sizable enough to support your lifestyle on a 5 percent annual return.

This is what making Millionaire Money Moves is all about and how it can lead to genuine transformation in your financial future.

INVESTING IN ENTREPRENEURSHIP

WHILE ENTREPRENEURSHIP IS THE SUREST AND MOST REWARD-
ing way to achieve Destination Millionaire, it's arguably the riskiest and
most difficult too. It requires all your creativity and strength and presents
some of the most complex challenges you may encounter in any aspect of
your life. Yet, in many ways, it gives you the best shot at achieving your
dreams, not only because it can result in great wealth, but because it will
unexpectedly help you uncover many talents you never even knew you
had. Remember how we talked about the "hero" character in Chapter 5 of
Why Should White Guys Have All the Wealth?? In entrepreneurship, the
hero is you. Depending on the type of business venture you're interested
in starting, and once you get your investment capital to Level 6 (between
$250,00 and $500,000) on my investment ladder, this could be the right
time to start your entrepreneurial journey.

When you own your own business, your income is only capped by the amount of work you put into it. In other words, you can make as much money as you're willing to work for instead of making as much as someone is willing to pay you. With a much higher income, you're able to invest at a level far greater than people who work a regular job. Over time, those exponentially larger investments will grow much larger as well.

Many folks mistakenly believe that the secret to being a successful business owner is to come up with a great idea. Ideas are important to be sure, but many clever ideas have died a lonely death in the absence of something even more important in business: a specific and valid need for that idea to fulfill. No matter what kind of business you decide to set up, if it can't address a need—even a need created through the magic of marketing—then all the money and hard work in the world won't ever lead it to success. That's why some of the smartest people fail at business, and some of the least likely characters end up becoming tycoons. Beyond that, entrepreneurship also requires sufficient funding (capital), expertise, and a little luck. Success in business ownership has everything to do with the demand for your goods and services and your ability to capitalize on that demand.

If it's true that "the road to hell is paved with good intentions," then the road to business success is easily one of the best-paved roads on the planet. Business failure is not only associated with entrepreneurship; it's practically its alter ego. But don't let that dissuade you. In fact, you can use that knowledge as a sort of armament for the challenges to come when you decide to open your own business. Since the odds are decidedly against your success, you can avoid being too critical of yourself and instead focus on the things that will make your business services and products fulfilling to others. If ever there were a formula for success in entrepreneurship, it might be this: expect small, but dream big.

BUSINESS OWNERSHIP FAILURE

How bad are your odds of success? According to data from the US Bureau of Labor Statistics, roughly 20 percent of small businesses in the US fail within their first year. By the end of their fifth year, about 50 percent have gone belly-up. Ten years on, only around a third of businesses will have survived. But fortunately, the reasons that businesses tend to fail are well known, the biggest of them being a lack of need in the marketplace, a lack of operating and/or expansion capital, and a poor choice of personnel. I speak from experience. I narrowly averted failure back in 2002 and again in 2003 when customers didn't want anything to do with what my business had to offer. Can you believe their arrogance? How could they not want what I had to offer?

That, my friends, is another reason why there is so much business failure. Arrogance doesn't happen in the marketplace; it happens in the mirror. We've all heard it said that the customer is always right, but so many of us struggle to accept this in business because we think we know better than our customers. Even brilliant entrepreneurs like the late Steve Jobs have made that mistake on occasion. In 1993, Apple came out with a digital assistant device called the "Newton." Virtually no one bought it, even though it was the electronic tablet of its day. But evidently, in 1993, people weren't interested or ready for that type of device. It became a laughingstock. Then in 2010, after years of careful development, refinement, and customization, Jobs took the stage again and publicly launched a new product called the iPad. Magically, millions of previously "arrogant" customers changed their tune and opened their wallets.

See what I mean? To be successful in business, you need to meet your customers where they're at, not wait for them to come to you. Thankfully for me, I was able to successfully pivot my business into something custom-ers wanted and then take the business to new heights. Business skills can be learned if you're willing to learn them. They don't require any special God-given talent. What's most necessary is an ability to find a need that you can fill and fill well. You don't need a "genius" idea; execution is in many ways as important as pure innovation. If you were to ask the owners of Burger King or Avis who invented the fast-food burger, or the rental car, they'd gladly tell you it was somebody else. Yet, they seem to have made pretty good money for themselves all the same. The most successful businesses find opportunities where others don't, then tailor themselves to meet that demand better than anyone else can. That's not to say that capitalizing your business and filling a need is in any way simple. It requires precise timing, an ability to turn on a dime, and a commitment to working like mad to capture that opportunity. Nights, weekends, and holidays become days like any other when your business is on the line. Entrepreneurship will test you mentally and physically and even when you give it your all, you will inevitably fall short at times. Yet, as you'll see, the journey of entrepreneurship is supremely worth it.

THE PROS AND CONS OF ENTREPRENEURSHIP

There's no limit to how much money you can earn as a business owner. You have control of your time and destiny, and you can pursue what you love as part of your everyday job. Business relationships are frequently rewarding and long-lasting as well and often form the basis of lifelong friendships. The only people you ever must report to are your customers. The boss has an easy-to-remember name too; you'll find it written on your birth certificate.

To go along with all those positive attributes, however, there are several reasons for which owning your own business can be fraught. The hours are demanding, particularly during the first several years of your business' life, and the hours will eat into family and relaxation time like sharks at a fish fry. Everything bad is your ultimate responsibility, whether it's your fault or not. That type of scrutiny and accountability is stressful, to say the least, and there will likely come a time when you feel lonely and isolated because few people other than fellow entrepreneurs have experienced that type of fear and stress themselves. Even if you're what's called a sole proprietor, you're likely to have people working for you, and the tasks of finding them, training them, keeping them, and managing them are not for the faint of heart. It's a mixed bag, to be sure, but in many ways the potential good so far outweighs the potential bad that deciding to become an entrepreneur is often a choice in name only, especially if you've suffered under the yoke of working for others.

STARTING A BUSINESS VERSUS BUYING A BUSINESS

There are two approaches to entrepreneurship; either buy an existing business or start one of your own. That choice may be dictated by your reason for wanting to become an entrepreneur in the first place. For instance, there may not be an existing business doing what you hope to do.

Although buying a business is almost certainly the fastest route to becoming an entrepreneur, fast isn't necessarily better. Nonetheless, when you purchase an existing business, you start with a customer/client base that's already in place. The same is true of employees, who will already be familiar with the business and how it works. An existing business has a track record, which can be a powerful asset in the rough and tumble of the competitive world of twenty-first-century commerce. Getting your foot into the marketplace can often be the hardest step of all.

On the other hand, retaining employees within the business you buy can be not only difficult, but, if unsuccessful, it can end up costing you the entire business. The margin for error is also much smaller when you buy an existing business. You may not have the time to learn all the subtle nuances before having to make potentially make-or-break choices. Another issue with buying a business is knowing the correct price to pay. You haven't been there to see if the advertised growth potential is realistic. And finally, the cost of accountants and lawyers to do proper due diligence on a business purchase can be prohibitive.

Starting your own business typically allows you to grow at a rate that you are comfortable with. You can design the business however you choose and operate it as you see fit. You only need a small bit of capital and minimal legal support to get started. You can even do it all electronically.

Much like raising children, though, the hard part comes after the moment of birth. Completing the certification process and obtaining approval as a minority or women-owned business enterprise, small business, or veteran-owned business is glacially slow. It takes time and additional money to set up a business' infrastructure and technology. Client acquisition is harder with a new business because you start without a track record, resulting in folks being less likely to purchase your goods and services at first. The same is true for acquiring funding from investors; they want to see proven progress, not promises of it.

Buying a business in a particular industry requires a deep understanding of the nuances of that industry and existing business relationships, which is why I believe it should be reserved for seasoned professionals who have gained that knowledge through specific industry experience. For our wealth-building journey here, let's focus on what it takes to get your own business off the ground and upward, toward the clouds.

CHOOSING THE RIGHT BUSINESS

Success in business begins with choosing the right business for yourself and for your product or idea. By "right," I mean a genuine business opportunity that's in line with your personal goals, financial aspirations, lifestyle, strengths, and constraints. A lack of this type of alignment makes it nearly impossible to succeed. Why? Because it too often causes a battle between your true self and your "idealized" self; a fight you're unlikely to ever win. Rather than working against yourself, you want to make a sober assessment of yourself and your circumstances and then choose the best and smartest business for you to create. There's a business that's right for you out there; that's a certainty. The question is what the criteria are to use to determine which one fits you. Here's a short litmus test with which to begin your search for the right business.

PASSION

Are you passionate about the nature of the work you'll be doing, the customers you'd be serving, or the goods and services that you'd be providing? People who don't like coffee, for instance, probably aren't cut out to open a specialty coffee shop. Even if they could run the business, why would they want to? There will be so many ups and downs, and your passion for the work must be able to fuel you when you get knocked down and question why you're even doing it (and question yourself, you will). Passion is a tricky criterion because following your passion doesn't always lead to making the kind of money you can live or retire on. If this is the case, you can always follow your passion philanthropically; just be sure to arrive at that decision before diving headfirst into owning a business you're passionate about that could never yield a profit.

TIME

How many hours and what days of the week or holidays are you willing to work in your business? If you cherish your weekends, evenings, and holidays, then businesses like restaurants, clubs, or retail stores may not be right for you. You must be honest about what time you're willing to dedicate to your business; otherwise, you'll end up inconsistent in your efforts, and your business will fail.

TALENT

You may think you have the talent to sing like Beyoncé. But are you a talented singer outside the shower, not to mention onstage? Do your family, friends, church parishioners, and music producers think you're talented? We often believe we have sufficient talent for something, and then we realize it's not enough after we try to start a music career or open the doors to our restaurant or consulting business. Self-belief is essential, but it's not enough to enable success in any business of your choosing, especially if your business is dependent upon customer or fan support.

SKILLS

No matter how talented you are, skills and training are required to enhance those natural talents. Training equips you to adjust to the ever-shifting seas of business ownership. When a business owner is both talented and skilled in their craft, the sky's the limit. You want to select a business for which you possess both characteristics.

EXPERIENCE

It's said that experience is the greatest teacher, so if you have experience in a particular line of business and you pay attention to that experience, you'll be able to skip many painful lessons. Experience will help validate your intuitions, provide credibility to your business offering, and assist you in starting a business capable of satisfying a genuine need in the marketplace. That experience often includes existing customer relationships and references who can open doors to business opportunities from the get-go.

LOCATION

Where your business is located matters. Location can be understood as both the physical location of your business, which is more critical for retail businesses that rely on foot traffic and street visibility, and its geographic location in relation to customers, employees, and suppliers. You must always consider the location of the people who will use your products and services, as well as the vendors you'll rely on to create and deliver your goods. You could decide to open a movie production company in Altoona, Texas, but if you need trained crews and access to film equipment, perhaps a place like Austin, Hollywood, or New York might be a smarter move. If your business relies on federal government contracts, why not set up at least some of your offices and facilities in Washington, DC? This would allow you to not only be close to where deals are made, but it could also facilitate your keeping an ear to the ground for other opportunities, conferences, or events related to your business.

While it's true that technology has made it far easier to operate a business from almost anywhere, business is still a contact sport. You must build and maintain relationships with key stakeholders to maintain and grow your business; otherwise, your competitors get the oyster while you get the shell.

Are you prepared to relocate yourself to open your business, or more to the point, if you could significantly increase the revenue and profit of your business by relocating, would you do it? If not, you may be going into the wrong business in your current location.

CAPITAL REQUIREMENTS

Access to capital is a common issue for entrepreneurs, and it's an especially acute problem for African American business owners. How much capital will you need to start your business? Have you written a business plan outlining how much it's going to take to start your business and operate it annually? Do you know how long it will take before your business can run on its own? Can you save up enough capital on your own and raise additional capital from friends and family, or are you going to need angel investors or venture capitalist money?

Considering the racial wealth gap between Blacks and Whites, why would we expect access to business capital to be any different? Some surveys estimate that Black businesses receive only 1 percent of venture capital in any given year. We can argue the wrongfulness of this another time. You have a business to get started, so you must remain focused on the things you can control. Most Black-owned businesses either fund themselves through personal savings, investment from friends and family, or through the (extremely risky) use of home equity.

You cannot start your business unless you can amass enough capital to last long enough for the business to become self-sustaining. If you don't have enough capital to start your desired business, then you'll need to get busy securing it *prior* to starting your business. I don't mean to be discouraging; I only wish for you to be realistic, so you'll have enough capital to successfully open and operate the right business and proudly hang your shingle for years to come.

NEED/DEMAND

Need and demand are possibly *the* most important criteria to apply to any business venture. Is there a genuine need for your business offering? Are there enough providers already satisfying this need, or is there adequate room for another provider in your business area? Have you done your research by talking with potential customers who can validate this demand? Do you know where your industry is headed and where demand for what you do is growing or contracting? How long will demand for your product and service last? Is your business idea a fad business, or will it be a way of life for the foreseeable future? There's no such thing as a crystal ball, but all these questions are not only valid; they're essential to ask and know in detail. There is nothing more frustrating than preparing for a business only to find out there is no real demand for your product or services. Markets shift before you know it, and you must be aware, willing, and able to pivot as demand shifts. It's important that you perform the necessary research in your industry; talk with potential customers and suppliers to validate that you're headed in the right direction.

CONTACTS/RELATIONSHIPS

Businesses are built on relationships. You'll need some reliable relationships with clients, vendors, and business partners even prior to starting your business. These are folks who can put you in the deal flow and help bring customers and opportunities to you. Always remember that they have relationships with other people too. A beauty supply store may have been buying their beauty supplies from the same supplier for twenty years. So, you must ask yourself, is your offering so much better that they'll be willing to forgo that relationship in favor of one with you? Maybe they'd save money if they went with you, but money isn't the only criterion in business. In fact, often what appears to be a question of money is a question of relationship, trust, and proven dependability. Sometimes a client or customer will pay more because they know their current supplier always delivers the right product on time. Therefore, be sure that, no matter which business you choose, you have enough relationships to get and keep the business up and running. Start by putting together a list of potential customers, business partners, and vendors whom you can go to for potential revenue and support. Then, determine if you have enough of the right contacts and relationships to start your business.

SOLUTION-ORIENTED

Does your proposed business solve a genuine problem in the marketplace? Unique solutions aren't compulsory, though they can be extremely helpful in selling and even demanding a premium for your offering. What too often happens, and this goes back again to the question of need, is that folks develop unique solutions to problems that don't need solving. It's known as the "Better Mousetrap" theory. Does the world need a better mousetrap, or does the one that's solved this problem for decades seem like it's still up to the task?

Most businesses are what I call "We Too" businesses; as in, we do what someone else does too. That's perfectly fine, though no matter what you do, you always want to be on the lookout for whatever will differentiate your offering from that of the others. Even if it's in your marketing alone (such as "Avis: We Try Harder").

INCOME AND PROFIT

Will your business idea generate enough income and profit? Can it help you to achieve financial independence or Destination Millionaire? Are the risks of time and money worth the reward? It's hard to earn a million-dollar profit running a single coffee shop or UPS franchise. As a potential business owner, you must be conservative when calculating the income potential of a business venture and determining if the stakes are big enough for the sacrifice. If not, you can easily end up working your tail off while barely making a living, which may not be sustainable nor help you in achieving your financial aspirations.

SCALABILITY

Scaling a business means enabling it to expand and grow. Can your business idea expand? Can you open it up in multiple locations? Are you willing to put in the extra effort required to scale your business? These are all big questions, and the answer to them can easily determine your fate as a business owner. If you've responded yes thus far, can you secure the capital necessary to scale your business, or in place of that, can it generate enough profit to grow organically? Although almost any business can scale, the managerial, human, and physical resources it takes to scale a business tend to be the bigger issues. You as the business owner must be able to find and hire the right talent to make that growth possible. If you foresee scaling your business as necessary to achieve your financial aspirations, then you need to take this last criterion into careful consideration beforehand.

EXIT PLAN

What will your exit strategy be? Are you planning to work until you're no longer physically able? Do you plan to pass the business on to your children? Are your children even interested in the business, and do they have or would they willingly develop the talent, skills, and experience necessary? Does your business have any saleable value? Perhaps you'll want to take your company public or sell it to someone else. If so, can you make enough profit in your business to achieve your endgame goals? You must be realistic with yourself. Most businesses have no saleable value. Think about it. Would you buy a hair salon, or would you build it? Would you buy a candle shop or create it? Someone might buy an established liquor store or a McDonald's franchise; the point is that you must run your business so that you are always increasing its value, but to do that, you have to know what value means to prospective buyers. Do you have inventory that can be resold? Do you have franchise agreements or an exclusive distributor relationship? Does your business own assets like real estate or patented products like software? These are only a few of the many questions to ask yourself about your long-term plan. You want to select a business that provides a path for you to exit on top.

Some businesses, such as restaurants, are great for making a living, but they consume so much of your energy that it's exceedingly difficult to scale them into multiple restaurants that might earn you a fortune. It's doable, but only with a great deal of effort and a lot of luck to boot. Whenever I consider starting or investing in a business, I'm looking to see how easily it can potentially scale and thereby increase my investment by orders of magnitude. Facebook is an excellent example of a small business that scaled into a multinational behemoth. Any of the major oil companies, such as Exxon, Shell, or BP, also started out small but scaled with certain ease because they had a product that was needed universally. Scaling means adding more customers, in more territories, with a constant array of new products or innovations.

You may have your sights set considerably lower. That's perfectly fine. Not every barbecue joint creator wants the headache of running fifty restaurants across the US, no matter how much they'd earn, though they might be happy to turn their famously delicious sauce into a scalable business sold in grocery stores. Some level of scalability is going to be required for anyone looking to create a legacy business because times and customs eventually change. For instance, while it's true there are some restaurants that have been around for eighty years, as a percentage of total restaurants over the last eighty years, they add up to remarkably few.

Now that you've evaluated and chosen the right business for you, it's time to take the next step of creating that business on your way to your endgame goal.

IDENTIFYING YOUR BUSINESS TYPE

Businesses typically create, distribute, transport, or resell products, or they sell or resell services. If you look at virtually every kind of business out there, you'll find some combination of those functions. By type, they look something like this:

- Manufacturing—Building products to be sold through retailers, wholesalers, and resellers (e.g., Pioneer, Apple, Whirlpool).
- Services—Providing services to businesses or consumers. Some service providers also sell products that complement their services (e.g., lawyers, doctors, consultants, hair salons, auto mechanics).
- Wholesalers—Selling and distributing products to a network of business partners either online, at retail, or to business resellers

(e.g., McLane Company—Groceries; Core Mark Holdings—Fresh, Chilled, and Frozen Merchandise; Eby Brown—Tobacco).

- Transportation—Moving equipment or transporting people by air (e.g., Boeing, American, Southwest), land (Amtrak, Greyhound, Uber), or sea (Carnival Cruises).
- Logistics—Distributing products from businesses to consumers or business to businesses (e.g., UPS, Federal Express, DHL).
- Reselling—Taking a product made by others and selling it (e.g., Best Buy, Walmart, Amazon, Target, etc.) to a customer base.

Over time, the nature of your business type may change. FedEx and UPS are good examples; they each began as shipping companies and later developed into logistics companies. Amazon...well, Amazon was a book-selling company that's now a media company, cloud service provider, logistics company, space transportation company, and much more. Why does this matter so much? Because if you don't understand your business identity, then you can't truly understand your business' capabilities and requirements. Take a company like Uber; if you only thought of it as a taxi service, rather than a transportation company, you wouldn't be able to see the areas of expansion they've successfully uncovered, such as food delivery and car, bike, and scooter rentals).

KNOWING YOUR BUSINESS MODEL

What does your business do? How does it operate? Who are your customers, and how will you serve them? How will the business make money? These questions and many others are answered by your business model. In essence, a business model is a description of how a company creates, delivers, and captures value for itself as well as its customers.

There are several types of business models, each with its own nuances, though here let's touch upon some of the ones you are most likely to encounter.

FRANCHISE

A franchise can be either a manufacturer, distributor, or retailer. Rather than creating a new product, a franchisee adopts the "parent" business model and brand and pays a royalty in exchange. Fast-food restaurants, such as McDonald's and Pizza Hut, are examples of franchise businesses.

BRICK-AND-MORTAR

Brick-and-mortar is the term used for a traditional business model in which retailers, wholesalers, and manufacturers deal with their customers face-to-face; in an office, a shop, or a store that the business owns or rents. Brick-and-mortar refers to physical space as opposed to an online or virtual one.

E-COMMERCE

The e-commerce business model is the modernization of the traditional brick-and-mortar business model. It focuses on selling products by creating a virtual web store online. Amazon is the world leader in e-commerce.

BRICKS-AND-CLICKS

This is a hybrid model in which a company has both an online and off-line presence, allowing customers to pick up online orders from the physical stores. This model provides flexibility and greater reach to customers who don't live in areas where the business has brick-and-mortar stores. Almost all apparel companies operate this way nowadays.

FREEMIUM

This is one of the most common business models on the internet. In it, companies offer basic services to their customers for free and then charge a certain premium for extras and add-ons. A freemium business offers multiple plans with various benefits for different customers. For example, the basic version of the file storage service, Dropbox, comes with 2GB of storage. If you want to increase that limit, you can move to the Pro plan and pay a premium price for it. YouTube follows a freemium model by offering content that comes with ads and other ad-free content for a premium. The freemium model is not only a great marketing tool but also a cost-effective way to scale up and attract new users.

SUBSCRIPTION-BASED

When customer acquisition costs are high, the subscription model can often be the most suitable option. The subscription business model allows you to retain customers over a long-term contract and get recurring revenues from them through scheduled repeat purchases. Netflix, Dollar Shave Club, and most newspapers and magazines are good examples of the subscription model.

ADVERTISEMENT-BASED

In this model, the customer receives products for free in exchange for being exposed to paid advertising. The more targeted exposure a business can deliver, the higher the rate it can charge to advertisers. Traditional television is the epitome of the advertising model; free programming is interrupted by paid advertisements. Sponsorship is another form of advertisement. Businesses charge other companies to associate their name with the product the business is selling, such as being "the official car" of the Olympics.

DATA SALES AND LICENSING

There's a saying in business that "if you can't see the product, the product is you." With the advent of the digital age, there has been a colossal increase in the amount of data generated by user activity on the internet. This has led to a new business model—the data sales and licensing business model. Many companies like Twitter and One Signal sell or license the data of their users—literally thousands of data points such as buying habits, search habits, demographic information, etc.—which the licensees then use to analyze and tailor their business offerings, customer acquisition strategies, mailing lists, and so forth.

NETWORK MARKETING

Network marketing or multi-level marketing is a pyramid-structured network of people who sell a company's products. The model runs on a commission basis where the participants are remunerated when they make a sale as well as when their recruits make a sale of the product. Amway is an example of a network marketing business model.

SOFTWARE, PLATFORM, AND INFRASTRUCTURE AS A SERVICE (SAAS, PAAS, IAAS)

Many companies offer their software, platforms, and infrastructure as pay-as-you-go services, whereby the customer pays only for their usage and the features they use, not the software, platform, or infrastructure. Adobe and QuickBooks are prominent examples of SAAS.

SHARING ECONOMY OR ON-DEMAND

In an on-demand model, a customer's order is fulfilled by delivering goods and services, usually immediately. Uber, Instacart, and Postmates are leading examples. The customer generally places their order through a web-based app, and the on-demand business coordinates and executes its fulfillment, whether by themselves or through third parties.

Choose carefully. Your business model will impact your go-to-market and advertising strategies, and it will also provide insights into several components necessary for creating a complete business plan, such as revenue segmentation, infrastructure requirements, key business relationship needs, and other factors required to successfully deploy and maintain the business model.

CREATING THE BUSINESS

It's relatively easy to set up a company in the US. Select a proprietary name, hire an attorney to assist you (the fees are generally quite reasonable), and choose an appropriate legal structure, such as C-Corp, S-Corp, Limited Liability Company (LLC), or Limited Liability Partnership (LLP). Your attorney and your accountant can assist you in determining which one best suits your business activities.

With some research and effort, you (or an attorney) will draw up what are called articles of incorporation and arrange for you to get a federal tax ID number, which is like a social security number for your business. You'll need to set up a separate bank account(s) for your business as well. Whatever you do, never mix your business records or finances with your personal ones. Ever. It can lead to severe and serious legal and tax consequences.

WRITING A BUSINESS PLAN

The advantages of having a well-drawn business plan are many. It not only shows you where you're headed, it provides a portrait of your business that outside investors or banks will use when deciding whether to provide you with capital investments. Think of your business plan as what you intend to do, how you're going to do it, how you're going to let your customers know what you're offering, and what you're going to achieve financially with the business.

A business plan helps clarify, document, and articulate your overall vision, which includes your business goals and strategy to start and operate the business. This is the document you'll use to share that vision with bankers, angel investors, venture capital firms, private equity firms, prospective executive-level employees, and advisory board members.

Why else do you need a business plan? Probably not for a reason you'd expect. There's no question that writing a business plan is hard work, and you may feel like you already know what your "plan" is, so why bother? Especially if you've got the gift of gab, you may wonder why you can't simply explain aspects of the business to anyone who asks. But while it's true that you will ultimately be sharing your business plan with others, believe it or not, for now your target audience is you. That's right; the person you're writing the plan for is the man or woman in the mirror. Here's why:

Your business plan says what you mean to do, and to know exactly what you mean to do, you must work out all the details to yourself in advance. If you can't clearly articulate to yourself things like what your goals and objectives are, what kind or amount of financing you may need, who you're going to sell your products or services to, or who and how many people you're going to have to hire to execute the plan, then how are you ever going to clearly convey that information to others? You must know from the get-go how you're planning to handle every aspect of starting and running your business, and the only way to be certain you do is to write it down and carefully review and revise your thinking. Your business plan is like that laminated play sheet that a football coach clings to during a game or the clipboard that a wedding planner carries around with her everywhere; the main difference being that you've got far more variables to address than both combined. Why would you do that sort of calculating in your head? It's all part of the necessary and sometimes tedious preparation every successful entrepreneur must do in preparation for their equivalent of the Big Game or the Big Wedding; call it the Big Livelihood if you like.

Is figuring out your business' technology, accounting, or real estate needs fun? I'll be honest: probably not. But if you don't figure them out now, you'll end up figuring them out under the gun and almost certainly at a greater cost. Luckily, there is an enormous silver lining to this kind of meticulous preparation that will pay dividends for years to come. It's called "confidence." There is a tremendous power in knowing every aspect of your business, down to the brand of flooring you use, and working it out in your business plan now means you will not only project confidence to others but feel it yourself when you most need it.

As an entrepreneur, you are the architect of your business, and beginning on day one, you need a set of blueprints to work from to build your vision. That's the role your business plan plays. When the time eventually comes for you to share that blueprint with others, whether they're outside investors, senior employees, or the loan officer at the bank, you will be able to present a clearly elaborated picture of the dream you wish them to be a part of.

There are countless resources on the shelves and online that go into detail on how to create a winning business plan. Our goal in this section is not to reinvent the wheel but to provide you with insights that can make that wheel roll a lot more smoothly.

A comprehensive business plan should include the following sections:

EXECUTIVE SUMMARY

An executive summary should not exceed five pages and should be a high-level overview of the main messages and points of your business plan. Make sure that the message and discussion points described in your executive summary are supported in detail by the information provided in the sections of your business plan. Keep this part simple. Say what your company does, why it will succeed, what products and services you're offering, and include your mission statement and, if you have one, a BHAG (Big Hairy Audacious Goal...an actual industry term). Examples of BHAGs are Microsoft's original, "A computer on every desktop," or Nike's BHAG from the 1960s, "Crush Adidas."

Give your plan's readers a sense that you've identified an area in the market that is not being served or is being underserved, while you've crafted a product or service that will meet the needs of that market. You should also include a financial overview of your revenue and profit goals over the next five years and why you're confident that your goals are realistic. Close with the amount of capital you're requesting and how and when you will be able to provide a significant return on the investors' capital. If your business plan is for a loan, explain when you expect to have the loan paid in full including interest and fees.

Be sure to include basic information about your employees, location, and the people on your leadership team.

BUSINESS DESCRIPTION

Write a company description that provides detailed information about your company, the market you are pursuing, and the problems your product or services solve.

Discuss the industry you are entering. Are you going to manufacture or distribute a product, work in the healthcare space, information technology, retail, government contracting, transportation, hospitality, etc.? Be specific, and list the consumers, organizations, or businesses your company plans to serve.

Identify your business type and model by referring to the sections on Identifying Your Business Type and Model above. Invoking a specific business type and model helps the reader clearly understand the business you are creating. Explain why you chose your business sector. Have you worked in this sector for many years and have a thorough understanding of the pros and cons of the sector? Explain to the reader why you're confident that you understand the problem and why you are uniquely qualified to provide a product or service to solve the problem.

Outline the size of the market in terms of revenue, and place it in its geographical context. Is demand limited to certain geographical regions, or is there a global need for your product or service? This will help the reader understand the scalability and long-range potential of the business. Show that you know your market and competitive landscape.

Explain the competitive advantages that will make your business a success. Are there experts on your team? Have you found the perfect location for your store? Your company description is the place to boast about your strengths.

ORGANIZATION STRUCTURE AND MANAGEMENT PLAN

The management and organization plan tells your reader how your company will be structured and who will run it. It describes the layers of your company and its reporting structure, who the CEO is, the vice president who will report to the CEO, the directors who report to the VPs, the managers who report to the directors, and the staff who report to the managers. Use an organizational chart to illustrate who is responsible for what in your company and show how the uniqueness of each person's experience will help guarantee your success (e.g., "Malcolm previously ran the software division at Google, one of our primary clients").

Show how your organizational structure will change as you scale at pivotal points over the next five to ten years. Most companies start out with a small number of employees, so in the early stages, this may not look all that sophisticated. However, I still recommend that, every year you're in business, you re-draft your organization chart and share it with your staff. As your needs for cash continue through your early years, a well-documented organization structure will come in handy.

Highlight your management team and include their bios and CVs, which should include details of their experience and education. The more talented the team you assemble, the more confident lending organizations will be in your ability to succeed. Also describe the legal structure of your business here (C-Corp, S-Corp, sole proprietorship, LLC, etc.).

TECHNOLOGY PLAN

We live and work in a digital world, and to succeed, every business needs *at minimum* a telecommunications plan, computers, internet access, a website, cloud-based applications to run the business (accounting, inventory, human resource systems, etc.), workplace collaboration tools, data management, storage tools, and a social media presence. Considering how critical an online presence has become, I highly recommend you invest a solid amount of money and care into making your website something special. It's so often the place where customers will first encounter and judge you, so you need to think of it the way you would an important meeting or a presentation to a room full of customers or investors, rather than a website that Cousin Bobby who's "kind of internet savvy" can set up for you. Ask yourself this: do you want to show up for your customers in your pajamas, or would you prefer to dress for success and shine?

You will need to determine if having a social media presence is critical to your business' success. My hunch is, it will be. If your products and services are intended to be offered to consumers, it is critical to have a plan to grow your social media followers and influencers. Some businesses like mine don't provide products or services to consumers; therefore, there is no ostensible need for us to have a social media presence. Nonetheless, a social media presence can help you attract high-quality young employees. Considering the growing power and ubiquity of social media, it probably makes sense to have at least some presence, no matter what type of business you'll be in.

SERVICES OR PRODUCTS OFFERED

Provide detailed drawings or service model diagrams to explain your business. Do you have intellectual property rights or patents that provide a competitive advantage over existing competitors or new entrants to the market? Make sure the reader has a crystal-clear understanding of your product or service offering. Explain why it's different and better than your competitors' and more in line with the current and future needs of your target customer(s). Does your product fill a need that's not yet evident, as Amazon did during the brick-and-mortar heyday of Borders and Barnes and Noble? If so, explain why you believe that the market will arrive where you're headed and when.

FIVE-TO-TEN-YEAR BUSINESS GOALS

It's difficult to project ten years into the future; however, in your business plan, you must at least project business goals for your first five years. That should include what product and service features you plan to deploy over that period to stay abreast or ahead of the market, as well as how much revenue that will add. Plans for expansion also belong here; what will your organization look like in years one through five? Expansion goals need to be accompanied by the projected costs of whatever expansion you're considering, including operating costs. Along with that, you'll want to detail items like additional office staff, office space, technology, accounting needs, and so forth. Here's where you begin to put the building blocks in place to create pro forma financials for the ensuing five to ten years (more on those in a moment).

Naturally, all your reasonable projections are based on a series of assumptions. Be sure to list those assumptions in this section so that the reader can follow your logic. They may not always agree with you, but at least they'll understand the basis of your projections. Think about your business' future in terms of what conditions must occur for it to achieve "X" dollars in revenue over the next five to ten years. Focus on market demand, product and service needs, and the costs of incorporating any future changes into your product offering. Each year can have its own dynamic set of assumptions; simply spell them out for each year, and roll with it.

MARKETING, ADVERTISEMENT, AND SALES STRATEGIC PLAN

There's no single way to approach a marketing strategy; it should evolve and change to fit your unique needs. Your goal in this section is to describe how you'll attract and retain customers. You'll also describe how a sale will eventually happen. You'll need information from this section when you prepare your financial projections, so make sure to describe your complete marketing and sales strategies.

When I think of marketing, I think of making a customer aware of an offering. Marketing may not necessarily make the sale, but it can create an awareness to countless potential customers so that they can take a closer look at what you're offering. Effective marketing involves geographically and demographically identifying your customers so that you create, design, and invest in targeted advertising campaigns that promote your product or service.

Your advertising strategy must both make your target market aware of your products and services as well as ignite a call to action (known as a CTA), which could be a request for more information or an actual sale. Social media has leveled the playing field in terms of enabling a small business to make a large customer base aware of their product and even generate a sale, though only to a degree. While the cost to advertise on social media can be as inexpensive as $50, it can also rise into the millions of dollars like traditional advertising. The leveling aspect is at the lower end of that spectrum because now nearly everyone can afford to do at least some advertising, thanks to social media. If you believe your marketing and advertising approach can benefit from social media advertising, make sure you share with your reader how you plan on leveraging and growing your social media capability.

As you might expect, your sales strategy needs to align with your marketing and advertising plan. Are there multiple sales channels where you focus on selling your products and services? Is there a retail store channel, an internet channel, a business-to-business channel where your customer is a business who then provides services to an end customer, or a business-to-consumer channel where your sales organization sells directly to the end consumer? Whatever your business' sales channels are, specify what percentage of revenue will be generated by each channel.

Any special relationships you or your business have go in this section as well. For instance, are you an authorized or exclusive reseller of a product? Do you have exclusive regional territory rights to sell or distribute a catalog of products and services? Are you a qualified or preferred vendor on many clients' vendor lists, or do you have personal relationships with client leaders who have agreed to do business with your organization? Remember to mention how these relationships will help to ensure your business' success.

COMPETITIVE ANALYSIS

To show your readers that you understand the competitive landscape of your market area, you need to prepare an analysis of your competitors. These are the four areas to address in your business plan:

1. A list of your competitors, what products or services they offer, where they operate, and their key customers. You need to show you fully understand your market and your competitors and you're not relying on hunches.

2. A distribution of your and your competitors' prospective market share, ideally in the form of a pie chart. What percentage of the market do they own, and what percentage of it do you plan to pursue? Be sure to specify if the target market is confined to a smaller region of the overall market, whether it's a city, state, group of states, or what have you.

3. A SWOT analysis of each of the top competitors in your market area. SWOT stands for Strengths, Weaknesses, Opportunities, and Threats. The goal is to carefully analyze what your competitor is offering so that you can identify potential opportunities to differentiate your products or services and capture market share. At the same time, SWOT will point you toward any potential trouble ahead, so you can adjust and fend it off. SWOT analyses are performed on a four-grid table that lists the information in each grid for the four analysis areas.

S.W.O.T. ANALYSIS

INTERNAL

POSITIVE

Strengths
Characteristics of a business that give it advantages over its competitors

Weaknesses
Characteristics of a business that put it at disadvantage relative to its competitors

NEGATIVE

Opportunities
Elements in a company's external environment that allow it to formulate and implement strategies to improve performance

Threats
Elements in the external environment that could endanger the business, its profitability, or its competitive advantages

EXTERNAL

4. A market differentiation table, which is the way to show What Makes You Special? Here's where you'll list your competitors along with their product and service features and show

how your offering is both different and better. I can't stress enough how important it is for you and anyone to whom you show your business plan to see that you're not simply a "We Too" business. Not only are you showing that your offering is superior to what's out there, but you're also demonstrating a keen understanding of the field you intend to out-compete. This gives a potential investor confidence that you know what you're doing and that their investment will be safe in your hands.

FINANCIAL PLAN

The financial plan must cover startup costs, a five-year revenue projection, operating expenses, net income, and your funding requests. Those requests should include a payoff plan or a convincing narrative as to how you'll increase investor value over those five years. This financial plan needs to be airtight and logical. The assumptions that drive your projections should be clearly outlined. Your goal is to convince the reader that your business plan is stable and will be a financial success.

If your business is already established, include income statements, balance sheets, and cash flow statements for the last three to five years. If you're seeking a loan and you have other collateral like a house or equipment that you could put against the loan, make sure to list it as well.

Provide a financial forecast for the next five years, including profit and loss statements, cash flow, and capital expenditure budgets. For the first year, be even more specific, and use quarterly—or even monthly—projections. Explain your projections clearly, and make sure they align with your funding requests.

STARTUP COSTS

It is always better to start your business using as little of your personal cash as possible. Preserve your left-over cash for personal needs or the needs of the business when it's critical. This is how you keep income coming through your door. When you eventually need another door, you can buy one with the business' profits. Countless are the entrepreneurs who have initially spent big money on showy offices, fancy cars for the leadership team, and pricey, ill-fitting technology, only to regret those decisions later. Don't make the same mistakes; do only what's necessary to keep startup costs low and revenues high. You want your plan to reflect a business that wears running shoes made for hustle, not gold slippers designed for waste. Here are some of the key practical issues you'll need to tackle:

OFFICE SPACE

What size office do you need for the first three to five years? Will you start out of your home office or basement, or do you need to rent a proper office or coworking space? Whatever you anticipate, be sure it includes enough space to accommodate your growth plans for the next three to five years, not the next fifteen to twenty years. All office expenses should be considered, including common area maintenance (CAM) costs that are typically added to tenants' rents at the end of each lease year.

Given the trend towards virtual work, you may be able to leverage savings by limiting how much in-person space you need to accommodate. Can your staff work virtually or from home? Do you have a large basement where you can set up a conference room for your staff to occasionally gather? This can save you handsomely on startup costs.

EQUIPMENT AND SUPPLIES

Computers, printers, file cabinets, desks, chairs, office supplies...these costs add up in a hurry and must be listed in your plan. One question to address is whether to lease or buy office equipment. I've always bought my office equipment and furniture, though that's simply a pet peeve of mine; I don't like renting anything unless necessary. Honestly, there's no perfect answer to the rent-versus-own question. From an accounting perspective, leasing lowers your taxable income more than the depreciation you receive by owning; however, you're on the hook to pay those leasing costs indefinitely. Purchasing equipment and furniture depletes cash flow, and the depreciation of it over time barely moves the needle on your business' taxable income. Also, business equipment becomes quickly obsolete, leaving little to no resale value to speak of. Ultimately, this is a personal choice. If you're more focused on the profitability of the business rather than the flashiness of it, consider buying used office furniture for your first several years. You'll find that it will cost you pennies on the dollar, and if your clients only come to your office on rare occasions, you'll be that much further ahead toward generating a profit.

PHONE AND INTERNET

Talk about an ever-evolving pair of technologies! Good internet service is a must in any business, as vital these days as electricity. Budget for excellent internet service from the outset in your plan; your business will surely come to depend on it. The good news for business owners about phones is that, for the most part, cellphones are no longer seen as "non-business" phones; plus, there is existing technology such as VOIP that can make even a cellphone feel more like a business line. Decide whether you plan to purchase or lease landlines. Ask employees to use their own phones; and plan to supplement their personal usage plans for business use.

LICENSES AND PERMITS

Business licenses and permits are usually not prohibitively expensive. As you account for any business licenses, permits, and incorporation fees needed to create your business, include the time it takes to obtain them if it will materially impact your ability to begin work.

INSURANCE

Business insurance is mandatory, with a minimum of liability insurance and healthcare for key personnel (and ideally, all employees). Don't guess-timate your business' insurance needs; speak to an insurance broker or provider, and include those costs in your startup calculations. Certain customers may require specialty insurance, such as Errors & Omissions or Umbrella Liability; if so, check that you're not over-insured, and consider pricing those extras into the cost of your services instead. You must stay on this regularly to make sure that you don't continue insuring clients with whom you no longer do business. The costs can be enormous. If you review and align your insurance needs annually, based on your current clients, you may find an opportunity to potentially lower your insurance costs.

To estimate your healthcare costs, call a local healthcare broker, and get quotes from leading healthcare providers. I'll forewarn you: it won't be cheap. This is a major line item; however, if you are going to attract and retain a quality workforce, you're going to need a good healthcare plan with all the bells and whistles. The initial cost may not amount to much, but the ongoing monthly premiums and annual increases will. Ask your broker for recommendations on how much of the premium you should cover and how much the employee should cover. You also must decide if the company is going to cover the same percentage for their families or if your company is only going to provide a percentage of the employees' healthcare cost while the employee covers their family's cost. Providing competitive pricing and healthcare benefits for your employees makes good business sense.

LAWYER AND ACCOUNTANT

Typically, your firm's legal counsel arranges the paperwork to form your business' legal entity. They also draft and conduct reviews on any agreements for your product, services, employees, and contractors. Your accountant initially sets up the chart of accounts and accounting system so that you can invoice your customers, pay your vendors, and run business performance reports. Get estimates from your lawyer and accountants for their services in advance, and remember, there are a lot of legal and accounting services that can be done more economically from offshore or middle-of-the-country service providers. They're generally able to provide the same services at a much cheaper price due to a lower cost of living in the Midwest and offshore. It's a common practice and reliable way of doing business these days, so explore these options before you commit. You may still need a local attorney who knows your state, county, or city laws, but there may not be a need to pay a premium for all your legal and accounting services. San Francisco Lawyers charge from $600 to $1,000 an hour for legal work. Lawyers in Minnesota charge $250 per hour for the same work. Why pay more for the same? Unless you're dealing with a serious local matter, don't waste the money.

INVENTORY AND SUPPLIES

Initial inventory is particularly important for product manufacturers, distributors, restaurants, and retailers, less so for service companies whose only inventory might be supplies for administrative support. Businesses need to pre-plan enough inventory and continue ordering inventory and supplies in advance of selling and distributing products. Truthfully, it's probably best to have more inventory than you need initially. Heaven forbid that you open your business and lose out on sales or have a customer lose faith in you because you don't have the products they need. I recommend planning for 10–15 percent more inventory than you need to keep the business running smoothly at the start. In time, you'll learn about your inventory turns and manage it flawlessly.

EMPLOYEE SALARIES

Employee salaries during the startup phase must be enough to cover the business from inception until you're generating enough profit in the business to fully cash flow it. This is always difficult to determine because you don't know how long it will take before the business breaks even. I recommend being conservative here. You want to have enough money to keep your team focused on building the business; if you don't allocate enough, you stand to lose the entire business before it ever truly gets going. Hopefully, you can negotiate with your team and consider offering them stock options in exchange for market-rate salaries. However, giving stock options should be a careful decision, and it will require additional legal fees to set up all the appropriate agreements.

Remember to put a salary in for yourself. You and your family have financial needs that must be met for you to be successful. Obviously, you need to trim down your personal financial requirements while you are starting your business, but starting a business thinking that you don't need a paycheck is a prescription for failure. Ideally, you want one to two years of salary available to pay yourself because success in a new business doesn't happen overnight. It takes time to get things running smoothly enough that you can draw a salary solely from the business' profits. For the first seven years of my business, I continued to consult at the client site for $175 an hour. I lived off a portion of my billable consulting rate and used the rest to cover business operating costs until the business got up and running smoothly.

In addition to salaries, you must pay payroll taxes which come to about 15 percent more than the cost of salaries. These taxes are for Social Security and Medicare, federal and state unemployment insurance, and workman's compensation. The rates vary according to the state in which your business is located. Overall, I recommend you budget enough money for salaries and payroll taxes to cover at least one full year of business expenses. If you're unable to fund your business for the first one to two years, you may want to consider delaying your start and raising more capital. Some businesses take years before they have a positive cash flow (e.g., Amazon, Uber), but the business plans for those companies were to capture market share before achieving profitability. Those types of businesses rely on several rounds of venture funding to keep them afloat. If this is the kind of business you're creating, make sure you can continue raising funds until the business takes off.

ADVERTISING AND MARKETING

Depending upon the type of business you select, your advertising and marketing costs can vary. By advertising and marketing, I mean marketing research, marketing material, brochures, letterhead, business card creation, and advertising creative, production, and placement.

In a service-only business such as mine, advertising and marketing won't raise much awareness or drive business to you. Service businesses are mostly relationship driven; therefore, advertising and marketing in a competitive bidding process to a buyer who already has a services partner, or who typically acquires service partners through their network, is pointless and a waste of money. Those clients are highly unlikely to respond to or be moved by an advertising campaign for your services, no matter how good it is, unless you're in the early stages of a new product offering. The type of advertising and marketing activity that *is* effective for a service business requires the personal touch of leveraging satisfied clients and customers who can refer you to their network of business leaders needing similar services. As far as the business plan goes for a services business, there's no need to allocate much money to advertising and marketing.

On the other hand, if you're in the manufacturing, distribution, subscription, or retail industries, marketing your products is essential to creating awareness among potential buyers. Your business plan should reflect a sizable budget to that end. How much money to allocate for advertising and marketing varies by industry and product, though it's usually calculated as a percentage of your annual sales. Do some research on your chosen industry to understand the appropriate percentage of sales to allocate for your marketing budget. For example, if you learn it's customary in your industry to allocate 5 percent of revenue to advertising and marketing and you anticipate $1 million in sales in your first year, then the amount you should allocate for Year 1 is $50,000. Be careful not to skimp; it will end up costing you more in the long run.

WEBSITE DEVELOPMENT

In today's business environment, a website is as essential as, if not more than, a business card. The cost to develop a website will range by the complexity of what you need and how you plan to use it. If you only need it as a marketing brochure, then you can get away with spending a few thousand dollars for a decent website. But if you need e-commerce features and a product catalog, then you're talking $20,000 and upward. Fortunately, website development services are increasingly available from less-expensive, offshore companies. Before you put a price into your business plan, solicit a few bids from local and offshore companies. Remember that there are other costs associated with setting up a website, such as choosing and paying for a domain name, a website hosting company, and sometimes a fee for the website builder framework (i.e., WordPress, WIX, Squarespace, etc.). Currently, these run anywhere from $4–40 per month.

SPECIALTY SOFTWARE SUBSCRIPTIONS

Back in the day, you could buy Microsoft Office or QuickBooks outright, including a license for every computer in your business, often at no additional cost. These days nearly all software is hosted in the cloud and paid for on a subscription basis. The good news is that you don't have to fork out a lot of money initially to get up and running. The bad news is you're on the payment hook for the foreseeable future.

Some businesses, such as mortgage, printing, and manufacturing, require costly specialty software. These must be included in startup costs as they are not optional. The same goes for any costs to hire consultants to set up and configure the software to meet your business needs.

Once you sum up all your startup costs, add an extra 10–15 percent contingency to the total in case you forgot or underestimated something.

It's better to have more than you need than not enough. Below is a real-life estimate of a mortgage business and how we estimated their startup costs. As you can see, we estimated a startup cost of $167,561.99. I also added $650,805.81 in operating costs for the first year, bringing our total startup capital to $818,367.80. We allocated another $500,000 in liquid cash to support our warehouse line of credit, used to purchase properties on behalf of buyers. This cash is never consumed; it remains in an account where the warehouse lender can place a lien against it so that it's always available. This is what's called liquidity in the mortgage lending industry. The warehouse line of credit is directly related to the amount of liquidity you maintain. Once Fannie Mae, Freddie Mac, or a mortgage servicing company approves our underwriting, they replenish the money in our line of credit so that we can underwrite new loans. Total startup costs to fund the business would've been $1,318,367.80. In the end, we pulled the plug for reasons that I will explain later, in the supplemental chapter on investing in Alternative Investments.

Mortgage Company
Estimated Startup Costs

Description	Costs
Lease	$9,862.00
License and Bond Fees	$699.99
Build-Out Costs	TBD
Accountant and Legal Fees	$5,000.00
QuickBooks License	$500.00
Computers and Printers (11 Laptops)	$11,000.00
Office Furniture (Desks, Chairs, File Cabinets, Dry Erase Boards)	$50,000.00
Encompass Implementation	$30,000.00
Phone and Network Cabling	$15,000.00
Conference Room TV, Projector, Camera, Microphones	$10,000.00
Network Switch, Server, and Rack Equipment and Installation	$5,000.00
Phone System Installation	$13,000.00
Website	$15,000.00
Letterhead and Business Cards Printing	$2,500.00
Launch Party	TBD
Total Startup Costs	$167,561.99
Operating Costs for the First 12 months in business (May 17-April 18)	$650,805.81
Total Capital Required	$818,367.80
Capital Reserved for Warehouse Liquidity	$500,000.00
Total Capital Required	**$1,318,367.80**

OPERATING COSTS

Operating costs are the annual and monthly expenses for everything the business needs to continue running, generating revenue, and earning a profit. Unlike one-time startup costs, operating costs don't go away and typically rise as the business grows. Knowing them helps you determine how much sales volume you need to cover your expenses and make a profit. Your business plan should include a list of business growth assumptions, such as staff increases, salaries, payroll taxes, office or plant space, and office furniture and equipment needed to support your growth. These increases should be included in your proforma or projected income statements so that you can explore the impact these costs will have on the business' profitability over time.

Mortgage Company Estimated Operating Costs

Expenses	1st Fiscal Year in Business [8 Months]		First 12 Months in Business		FY 2018	
Rent	$19,793		$44,517		$44,517	
Salaries & Fringe	$171,542		$478,975		$1,078,700	
Software Services	$15,900		$26,200		$31,800	
Phone and Copier Leases	$11,992		$11,992		$25,968	
Internet and Phone	$3,519		$3,519		$14,076	
Office Supplies	$1,395		$1,395		$5,580	
Business Insurance	$3,250		$3,250		$13,000	
Health and Disability Insurance	$27,269		$68,450		$126,882	
Marketing, PR, and Advertising	$0		$0		$0	
Professional Services [Legal, Audit]	$10,000		$10,000		$15,000	
Postage/Mailing Fees	$375		$875		$1,500	
Bond Expense	$375		$875		$1,500	
State License and Fees	$325		$758		$1,300	
		Avg. Monthly Operating Exp.		Avg. Monthly Operating Exp.		Avg. Monthly Operating Exp.
Total Expense	$265,734	$26,573.42	$1,905,808	$54,233.82	$1,359,823	$113,318.58

The table above reflects the operating expenses for that same mortgage company in which I was looking to invest. Many of these expenses are standard to any business. Notice that there's no budget provided for marketing and advertising; that's because I was waiting for input from my partners, the mortgage industry experts, but they never provided it—a definite red flag! In the table, I estimated the first eight months of operating expenses, twelve full months of operating expenses, and fiscal year (FY)

2018 operating expenses. I did this because we were starting out in May of 2017 and therefore would only have eight months' worth of expenses in that first calendar year. The remaining column shows twelve full months of business operation costs. This allowed us to see what a full year of operation looked like to validate our assumptions about revenue goals and ensure that we could positively cash flow the business as we ramped up.

Naturally, the operating expenses for your business will look different, though you can use this example as a guide. Be sure you have a realistic understanding of how much money you'll need to run your business smoothly prior to and after you've launched it.

THREE-TO-FIVE-YEAR PRO FORMA FINANCIAL STATEMENTS

This is a three-to-five-year projection of the business financials, which includes a profit and loss statement, balance statement, and cash flow statement. This three-to-five-year outlook is based on a set of assumptions about the business that owners use to drive their projections. While not 100 percent predictable, they should closely represent how the business is expected to perform. The quality of the assumptions is key, and savvy outside investors will recognize which of your assumptions are reasonable and which are not. Therefore, don't guesstimate; put serious thought into your assumptions because you will be questioned about them when you present to potential investors. Let's look again at that mortgage business and see what those assumptions looked like:

- Each branch of the business would add 40 percent to the overall baseline operations cost for additional underwriters, shippers, compliance, and management support.
- Loan offers would be commission-only employees.

- Loan officer commissions would be 40 percent of the fees to the business.
- After FY 2018, each loan officer would be closing an average of three loans per month.
- Each branch manager would maintain at least sixteen active loan officers per branch.
- Each branch would generate $5,148,000 in annual revenue from loans.
- We would open four new branches every six months.

From those assumptions, we modeled a five-year revenue schedule for the business.

Projected 5-Year Mortgage Revenue By Branch Office

Branch Locations	LOs	2017 Loan Volume	2017 Revenue	2018 Loan Volume	2018 Revenue	2019 Loan Volume	2019 Revenue	2020 Loan Volume	2020 Revenue	2021 Loan Volume	2021 Revenue
Main MA ATL Branch	10	30	$193,500	840	$5,418,000	768	$5,148,000	768	$5,148,000	768	$5.148M
LA ATL Branch	15					768	$5,148,000	768	$5,148,000	768	$5.148M
AA ATL Branch	15					768	$5,148,000	768	$5,148,000	768	$5.148M
MD AA Branch	15					192	$1,296,000	768	$5,148,000	768	$5.148M
FL LA Branch	15					192	$1,296,000	768	$5,148,000	768	$5.148M
FL LA Branch	15							384	$2,574,000	768	$5.148M
MD MA Branch	15							384	$2,574,000	768	$5.148M
TX LA Branch	15							384	$2,574,000	768	$5.148M
TX AA Branch	15							384	$2,574,000	768	$5.148M
DE AA Branch	15									384	$2.574M
VA MA Branch	15									384	$2.574M
MD Branch	15									384	$2.574M
NJ Branch	15									384	$2.574M
Total	190	30	$193,500	840	$5,418,000	2,688	$18.036M	5,376	$36.036M	8,448	$56.628M
Growth Percentage			0.0%		2,700.0%		232.9%		99.8%		57.1%

Using our deployment schedule, we projected the number of loan officers and showed when they would begin contributing revenue to the business. Loan volume assumed that each loan officer would produce three loans per month. From these two metrics, we were able to predict our revenue from 2017 to 2021.

With these revenue projections and the operational costs in hand, we could prepare the three-to-five-year pro forma income statement. The table below represents our pro forma income statements for the first five years in business. Note that our first year is only eight months while the remaining years cover a full twelve months.

Proforma 5-Year Profit/Loss

Revenue	1st Fiscal Year 2017 in Business (8 Months)		FY 2018 at 3 Loan per LO Monthly		FY 2019 at 4 Loan per LO Monthly		FY 2020 at 4 Loan per LO Monthly		FY 2021 at 4 Loan per LO Monthly	
Loan Orig. Fees	$193,500		$5,418,000	$451,500	$18,036,000	$1,503,000	$36,036,000		$56,628,000	
Direct Loan Costs										
Loan Officer Commissions	$77,400		$2,167,200	$180,600	$2,167,200	$601,200	$14,414,400	$1,201,200	$22,651,200	$1,887,600
Gross Profit Margin	**$116,100**	$11,610	**$3,250,800**	$270,900	**$3,250,800**	$901,800	**$21,621,600**	$1,801,800	**$33,976,800**	$2,831,400

Expenses	1st Fiscal Year in Business (8 Months)		FY 2018		FY 2019		FY 2020		FY 2021	
Rent	$19,793		$44,517		$57,872		$151,358		$204,778.20	
Salaries & Fringe	$171,542		$1,078,700		$1,402,310		$3,667,580		$4,962,020	
Software Services	$15,900		$31,800		$41,340		$108,120		$146,280	
Phone and Copier Leases	$11,992		$25,968		$33,758		$88,291		$119,452.80	
Internet and Phone	$3,519		$14,076		$18,299		$14,076		$64,749.60	
Office Supplies	$1,395		$9,765		$12,695		$33,201		$44,919	
Business Insurance	$3,250		$13,000		$16,900		$57,460		$59,800	
Health and Disability Insurance	$27,269		$126,882		$164,947		$431,399		$583,657.20	
Marketing, PR, and Advertising	$19,350		$541,800		$1,803,600		$3,603,600		$5,662,800	
Professional Services (Legal, Audit)	$10,000		$15,000		$19,500		$51,000		$69,000	
Postage/Mailing Fees	$375		$1,500		$1,950		$5,100		$6,900	
Bond Expense	$375		$1,500		$1,950		$5,100		$1,500	
State License & Fees	$325		$1,300		$1,690		$4,420		$5,979.82	
Total Expense	$285,084	$35,636	$1,905,808	$158,817	$3,576,810	$298,068	$8,220,705	$685,059	$11,931,837	$994,319.72
Total Profit	-$168,984	-$21,123	$1,344,992	$112,083	$7,244,790	$603,732	$13,400,895	$1,116,741	$22,044,963	$1,837,080.28
	-87.3%		24.8%		40.2%		37.2%		38.9%	

You can see that in our first year we were set to lose money because our first eight-month costs are high relative to our ability to generate revenue out of the gate. That's a realistic portrayal of a likely outcome. Investors are smart; few of them obtained large sums of investment capital by being naive about how businesses work. So, don't try and fool them into thinking you're going to make a boatload of money in the first year. You will lose credibility, and they will likely walk away, taking their trust in you along with them. Investors prefer realistic and conservative projections; they would rather you under promise and overdeliver than do the opposite.

Beyond the pro forma income statement in your business plan, you'll also need to provide the associated balance sheet showing how the business' assets, liabilities, and owners' equity will change over the same three-to-five-year period. The same goes for cash flow statements, which will show that your business will have enough cash in the business to operate efficiently and meet its cash obligations in a timely fashion. This is a great place in your business plan to use graphs and charts to highlight the financial story of your business and demonstrate that you'll have sufficient cash flow to keep the engines running at full speed.

Given the supreme importance of this section of your plan, I recommend you consult with a CPA to help create high-quality financial projections and statements. You'll need this part of your business plan to be airtight to garner serious attention from investors and bankers. Also, remember to add the cost of accounting assistance for your business plan to your startup cost estimate.

FUNDING REQUEST

If you're asking for funding, use this section to specify whether you seek debt or equity financing, your ideal debt or equity terms, and either the length of time you'll need to pay back the loan or the date when investors will be able to cash in on their increased equity. Give a detailed description of how you'll use the funds. Do you need them to buy equipment or materials, pay salaries, and cover specific bills until revenue grows to certain levels? Always include a description of your long-range business goals, such as expanding the business to whichever level you see fit, going public, merging with a competitor, or selling the business for what you think it will be worth at a future date.

BUSINESS PLAN DEVELOPMENT ASSISTANCE

Creating a business plan will require you to do some grunt work, such as market industry and competitor research as well as financial projections. (I told you becoming an entrepreneur would be hard.) Don't let that hard work dissuade you; the payoff that awaits is well worth it. Take advantage of the wealth of excellent free resources online. The US Small Business Administration (SBA) website, for one, offers templates for a business plan, as well as specifications on length and what to include. There are also organizations that provide in-person help with your business plan, such as the experts at SCORE (Service Corps of Retired Executives), a nonprofit network of more than ten thousand volunteers willing to serve as expert business mentors. You may even choose to hire a freelance business plan consultant who can walk you through the process of writing a winning business plan.

ACQUIRING CAPITAL FOR YOUR BUSINESS

There are six main sources of capital out there to fund your business. They are personal savings, friends and family, community development organizations, financial institutions including banks, angel and venture capital investors, and most recently, crowdfunding. Personal savings and/ or friends and family have been the most common ways that African American business owners have funded their business. Historically, only about 1 percent of African Americans have received funding from venture capitalists, though since the tragedy of George Floyd's murder, more capital is being made available to African American entrepreneurs from banks and financial institutions, as well as angel investors and venture capitalists.

PERSONAL SAVINGS

The most common source of business capital for Black entrepreneurs is personal savings.[4] This is why M$M focuses on showing you how to increase your earnings and lowering what you pay and consume, so you can generate the money needed to invest in a business if entrepreneurship is one of your paths to Destination Millionaire and beyond. I derived the startup capital for my business from personal savings. In retrospect, it was one of the best decisions I ever made. You don't want anyone breathing down your neck if you can avoid it, especially as you make your way through the ups and downs of business ownership. It's a tough enough road to travel without having capital shortfalls or debt service to add to the pressure.

The challenge with relying on your personal savings is that it takes time to build enough of it to fund your business, and if the business should fail, you'll risk exhausting all the cash reserves it's taken you years to amass. At a minimum, you'll need sufficient capital to cover your personal expenses as well as the business' startup and operating costs for the first year or two to have a fighting chance at survival. Since you must make a sizable investment to get started—long before you can make a profit from your goods and services—you're likely to lose money at first. You and practically every other business in the world, that is. Try not to let it dissuade you; it's simply a part of the process. If two years' initial funding is too much

---

[4] "Black Entrepreneurs 2021," Guidant Financial, accessed June 15, 2022, https://www.guidant financial.com/small-business-trends/african-americans-in-business/.

for you, you can make a go of it with only one, though your window for long-term survival will shorten along with it.

FUNDING FROM FRIENDS AND FAMILY

Friends and family can also be a reliable resource to draw upon for startup funding, but bear in mind that, due to the generational wealth gap in the African American community, not all entrepreneurs of color can turn to their loved ones to help fund their businesses and get them off the ground. If you can secure financial assistance from friends and/or family, be sure to treat them with the same diligence and respect as you would any ordinary investor. Share your business plan with them. Write out and provide a detailed repayment plan and schedule if they're loaning you money, as well as the rate of interest you agree to pay. If they're investing in exchange for equity, have an attorney prepare appropriate agreements that lay out the terms, including the number or percentage and type of ownership shares they're buying in your firm. Any progress reporting you plan to give investors must be given to *all* investors, whether they're related to you or not.

In my business dealings, I've shied away from investments or loans from close friends or family because I prefer to shield my friendships from my business affairs. If you can't do that outright or wish to operate differently, cement your agreements with careful paperwork so that investment issues with friends or family don't come up at Thanksgiving dinner. You'll need to consult with your accountant as well because even gifts from friends or family are limited by rules and subject to taxation. If you're serious about getting your entrepreneurial idea off the ground, it's going to require you to use some of your own capital—what is commonly called having "skin in the game"—to get started, along with any capital from your friends and family, whose love and belief in you replaces any need for proof of past success.

FUNDING FROM COMMUNITY DEVELOPMENT AND NONPROFIT ORGANIZATIONS

There are also several business grants available to help fund startups. They're called Community Development Financial Institutions (CDFIs) and presently range in value up to $5,000 per business. They're awarded to businesses who participate in business plan or business "elevator pitch" competitions. Although these grants are small, they can help you boost your personal savings that you use to fund your business. Other nonprofits such as Accion provide funding to startup businesses as well. Look around, and take advantage of free money however and whenever you can. It's not charity; it's the smart thing to do.

FUNDING FROM BANKS AND FINANCIAL INSTITUTIONS

Banks and other traditional lenders make loans available to businesses although they typically require you to be up and running for at least three to five years or put up collateral against the loan (in the form of a home equity loan, for instance). Your credit score needs to be on point as well, 650 or above, to secure their loans. Banks don't like to take big risks. Using your home as collateral is a viable way to secure the cash needed for your business, but know that it's highly risky. If your business doesn't get off the ground, you could lose your home and your business and cause significant suffering to your family. So, be extremely careful.

As I mentioned, in the wake of the George Floyd tragedy, banks have begun to invest billions of dollars in private equity and venture capital funds that focus on providing capital to Black-owned-and-operated businesses. This has been especially helpful to startups without long-standing track records.

It may take you, as it often does, a combination of personal savings, friends and family support, bank loans, and community grants to raise enough money to start your business. But someway, somehow you must get there. If you're still coming up short, you can always seek out an angel investor or a venture capital firm, though this is where things get a bit more complicated.

FUNDING FROM ANGEL INVESTORS AND VENTURE CAPITAL FIRMS

Angel investors and venture capital firms are two of the most powerful catalysts for turning a startup into a goldmine. An angel investor is exactly what it sounds like—a wealthy person who believes in your idea and funds it with a sizable check in exchange for equity in your business. The "sharks" of *Shark Tank* are angel investors, at least by definition. Venture capital comes from companies set up to invest in businesses (such as a tech or biotech company) who've got off the ground and now need to expand. Many of these firms have been founded by entrepreneurs who enjoyed enormous success with their own ideas, such as the Winklevoss twins, who helped create Facebook, or Marc Andreesen, inventor of Netscape, the first widely used internet browser.

There's a common misconception that angel investors and venture capitalists have so much money that they don't blink at writing the next check to a startup because they can so easily tolerate a loss or write it off on their taxes. That's a belief that belongs in the deli section, under "SPAM." The idea that all we need to do is scribble our business plan on a napkin and a willing investor will magically appear and hand us money to start our own company is plain foolishness. Instead, with the right mix of diligence and proper planning, successful fundraising for your business is out there for the taking.

The key concept to grasp is that millionaire investors who can help fund your business are—like you—risk takers, not gamblers. The overwhelming majority of millionaires build their money slowly and therefore greatly value what they've built. They're not looking to lose their capital. Think about it; if an investor were to give you money based solely on an idea that you drew on a napkin, that'd be a big gamble, *unless* you already had a track record of success a mile long. Therefore, smart investors do their due diligence; they need to know you possess the ability to be successful. They need to see your track record. They need to see your hustle. They need to see your resourcefulness and your resilience. Do you have enough determination to get the business started and prove your business model works? Has anyone else given you money that's led to a sizable return on investment (ROI) for them? Do you have a business plan that an investor can understand and believe in? Can you clearly articulate how and when you're going to make money on your business? Can you demonstrate to the investor when they will receive their initial capital back and more?

Any serious investor will need you to address these criteria and likely several more. If you don't possess a track record in business—and there's no sin in that—VC investors are unlikely to come in until you've first proven your business can make money. Once you can demonstrate that your business works, you'll be able to successfully solicit new investors in exchange for equity ownership in your company. You don't want to make the mistake a friend of mine made. While a lovely guy, he would often go on about how one day he'd find someone to invest in his food truck, then get a loan, then build a bigger business, and so on. Here's what's wrong with that type of thinking; outside investors want you to prove that your model for growth is viable *first*. Proof of concept is essential to getting others to invest in you. You need to show not only that your business works but that the growth of your business works too. Think of it this way: whatever it is you're selling, your job is to go from selling, proportionally speaking, one unit to five units. Your investors' money is to help you get from five units to a thousand units, five thousand units, fifty thousand units, or as high as the model can grow. You can't come walking in with sales at one unit and say, "See! Isn't this great? Give me money, and I bet other people will want to buy more of my product or service."

I deliberately wrote the word "bet" just now because it's a gambler's term. Try saying "bet" to the next serious investor you meet, and see how fast they walk out the door. What they want to hear is, "Here's concrete proof that my product sells. In a short time, it's already grown by a factor of five. This shows that my business model works." I'm not saying that a factor of five is the magic bullet that will unlock investment, though; I am saying that proof of concept almost always is. That proof comes in many forms and at many numerical valuations. Once you start investing and begin to grasp the ways of the marketplace, you will better understand how to recognize growth patterns in your own endeavors.

Study your business, study your potential investors, and prepare to show them materially that you're a worthwhile risk, not a gamble. Have your business records in order, your employees (if you have any) in place or standing by and vetted for hire, your operating procedures documented and standardized, and your vision for the business' future succinctly focused. Your charm and enthusiasm may get you in the door, but only your preparation and financially sound proof of concept can get you back out that door with new investment capital in hand.

CROWDFUNDING

Though a relatively recent phenomenon, crowdfunding has firmly taken hold as a viable way of obtaining capital for your business; anything from a new tech startup to a novel rehab program to treat addictions.

Crowdfunding is exactly what its name purports to be; individual investors form a "crowd" of investors until a funding goal is reached. In exchange, investors can receive equity in the businesses they partially fund or something as simple as a shout-out and an invitation to a company event in the future.

There's no hard and fast rule to incentivizing funders, though with a little research, evolving trends can be identified and mimicked. There's also no limit to how much can be raised through crowdsourcing, nor what can be offered cash for equity, loans for businesses, or even straight donations. Thus far, billions—yes, billions—of dollars have been crowdfunded with an ever-expanding number of crowdfunding sites coming online every year.

Here are some of the leading sites worth exploring:

- Kickstarter
- Indie GoGo
- Crowd Finder
- Experiment
- Chuffed
- Crowd Supply
- Fundable
- Patreon
- Fundly

Should you choose to seek funding from a crowdfunding source, you'll need to prepare a business plan and a "pitch," typically in the form of a video about your product or idea and, equally important, yourself. Crowd funders are no different than other angel investors; the people they invest in matter as much as the business ideas themselves. Each of these sites contains helpful information about how to best tailor your pitch to their brand of investors. You may be adept at producing a high-quality video on your own, but if not, spend a little money and hire a professional. You'll need to put on your best face to win over investors, and your pitch video is your one and only chance to get that crowd investing in you.

SETTING BUSINESS GOALS

How you run your business means how you operate the day-to-day activities to manage and grow revenues, lower costs, and increase your profits. Some folks confuse merely showing up at the business with running it, but unfortunately, businesses don't run by themselves. Every entrepreneur needs to set business goals, execute on those goals, track performance, and navigate the many challenges and setbacks that arise in the life of a business.

As discussed, your business goals should be initially established as part of your business plan and updated annually thereafter. Ideally, you'll want to establish at least a five-year high-level strategic plan and annual business goals that align with it. As with personal wealth-building goals, I feel that planning a business beyond five years is not only challenging but often pointless because so much can change. Unless you have an unusually longtime horizon for product development (such as a new drug or something like space technology), five years is more than sufficient for you to project into the future.

The thrust of your business goals should be revenue growth, cost containment, increased profitability, add-ons, or innovations to the product or service offering and maintaining and growing market share. The criteria that make up that specific vision will indicate any changes you must make in your talent pool, infrastructure, sales, management team, or plans for innovation. You'll also have a window into your long-term and annual operating costs, which is essential to determining how much revenue will be required to achieve whatever profit goals you establish. A five-year, high-level strategic plan should answer the following questions:

- What should our year-over-year sales goals be?
- How much volume can we reasonably expect to sell and at what product or service mix, year-over-year for the next five years?
- What price point do we set for our products and services to support our sales volume, revenues, and operating expenses?
- How many clients, estimates, and proposals in the pipeline do we need to achieve the sales revenue targets for each of the five years?
- How much do we need to spend on marketing and advertisements to achieve our five-year sales goal?
- What talent and personnel will we need, and how will any additional staff impact overhead costs?
- How will our infrastructure needs and costs be affected (office or workspace, equipment, software, etc.)?
- How will our operating costs be impacted year-over-year by the five-year vision?
- What additional capital is required to fund our vision, and how will we obtain it?

A well-thought-out set of goals addresses these questions and more. It also ensures that your business can grow large enough to earn the profits which will allow you to achieve your endgame, whether you plan on selling the business down the road or simply stack up your profits until you've reached your financial destination.

EXECUTING ON YOUR BUSINESS GOALS

Having a plan is one thing, but executing your plan is everything. Plan execution is the hardest part of the process, and you simply can't succeed if you fail to execute. In the workplace, it's common and all too easy for businesspeople to emerge from their standing Monday morning meetings all fired up, only to lose sight of or even forget the business' weekly goals by about Tuesday afternoon. I speak from experience. Rah-rah alone ain't gonna do it. In my company, we have a standing Monday morning meeting in which all departments are required to communicate the focus of the next two weeks. I strongly urge you to do something similar, and even more. To keep us on track through the rest of the week, my management team has an agenda that maps directly to our strategic plan. Whether you're operating a software company or a string of laundromats, the methodology and importance remain the same. If you adhere to this kind of structured discipline when the company is small, it will be much easier to manage your growth going forward. Size matters, but process matters as much or more. If you implement and practice the right processes now, it will be much easier to scale that across your business empire as it expands. If you don't, your success can easily end up overwhelming you and your staff.

TRACKING BUSINESS PERFORMANCE

Businesses have so many moving parts that the only way to stay on course is to always know your current position. This requires a consistent procedure for monitoring performance—in other words, an early warning system to alert you before you veer too far off track. You can then make the necessary adjustments—in time—to achieve your business goals. In my business, we call it our quarterly business review (QBR) process.

I start each business year with an annual kick-off meeting outlining the business goals for the year: revenue goals, costs goals, consultant growth goals, how we're going to improve business functions like IT, HR, and so forth. At the beginning of each year, our sales, delivery, operations, and administrative department heads create quarterly goals designed to move the business forward. At our QBRs, each department head is required to present a status report on the current year's strategic business initiatives and goals. Our sales team provides a sales pipeline presentation of how the sales team is performing, as well as the status of pending deals, future deals, and the likelihood of us reaching our revenue goals. That pipeline is reviewed twice a month so that we can monitor the activities of our sales team and accurately predict future sales outcomes.

In addition to conducting QBRs, I do a weekly review of our financial statements (profit and loss, balance sheet, cash flow statements, aging receivables, and aging payables), which are prepared by my Chief Financial Officer (CFO). I have both a revenue and cost report provided to me every month which gives me insight into how the business is performing as well as any meaningful trends. The purpose of all this tracking and reporting is to spot issues before they become problems. Whenever trouble arises, each of our department heads is responsible for presenting recommendations to course correct. Your specific approach to accountability will undoubtedly differ. What matters is that you have a way to regularly see, measure, and respond in a timely fashion to how your business is performing in relation to its established goals. You simply can't leave it to chance if you plan on succeeding.

GROWING THE BUSINESS

The primary objective in business ownership is to increase overall value by constantly increasing earnings and market share. The simplest way to increase your EBITDA (a key valuation acronym which means earnings before interest, taxes, depreciation, and amortization) is to increase your sales volume, revenue, and/or profit margin while keeping your costs relatively steady. You can also try reducing costs by offshoring certain tasks or manufacturing your products with less expensive materials, so long as you maintain at least the same quality that your customers expect. Another way to increase EBITDA is to dramatically lower operational costs by reducing your rent, IT costs, HR costs, healthcare costs, and so forth. Honestly, though, you may find that unless you dig in and work hard at it, there's not a great deal of savings to be found this way. One other approach to grow market share and increase revenue and profits is to expand your customer mix and offer new products and services. You may also consider acquiring a competing firm. No matter how you approach the task, always be looking for ways to grow your business and its valuation because if you're not growing the business, chances are you'll soon be going out of business.

HIRING AND RETAINING PERSONNEL

One of the most, if not *the* most, difficult parts of small business ownership is attracting and retaining personnel. It seems like no matter what you do or how hard you try, successful hiring either remains elusive or your great new hire walks out the door just when you think you got things right. Either your new hire doesn't represent your business appropriately, or if they do, they get recruited away by a larger, more established company, an exciting startup, or one of your competitors...after you've trained them and invested significantly in their development.

One big reason why hiring and retaining personnel is hard in business is because the exciting tech companies like Apple and Google tend to attract a giant swath of A-caliber employees, while the IBMs and Johnson & Johnson's of the world scoop up their share of the A- and B-caliber employees, and on it goes down the line. Small bootstrapping startups without celebrity VC investors tend to entice, well, let's say a lower tier of employees. I'm not saying there aren't As and Bs among them; it's just that the pickings are slimmer. Naturally, whether your company is large or small, your clients and customers will still demand and expect A-caliber effort, work, and results. Hence, the pickle that small business owners find themselves in, talent-wise.

In the wake of the COVID-19 pandemic, today's workers want all the bells and whistles: big compensation, unlimited paid time off, paid sabbaticals, remote work—you name it. And in many instances, they're getting it and more. This adds to the difficulty for new, small businesses when competing for good employees, especially if a company's prospects for growth are, at least for the time being, modest at best. So, if you're not the next Apple or Google, my advice is this: don't try to compete with them. You do you. Whereas large established companies can offer great benefits, a small company has a secret formula that's too often underutilized. It's called "a sense of belonging." For all the amenities today's workers are seeking, they are also overwhelmingly looking for greater meaning in their jobs. The intimacy and close-up view of your business, plus a healthy dose of tangible camaraderie, may be more important to them than an extra week off each year. You never know.

In any event, finding and keeping good talent will always be a challenge in any business. People lose interest, get more enticing offers, or change career paths without you even knowing until it's too late. Here are a few best practices for your business to help you navigate your hiring and retention challenges:

LEVERAGE YOUR PERSONAL NETWORK

The best place to start when you're building your team is your personal network. These are business colleagues from current or past employers who work in the same industry as you, are excellent at what they do, and can complement your skillsets. Often, these folks are hard to recruit unless they see a significant opportunity to get rich with you. To attract them and bring them on your team, you may have to offer them some shares in the company. If you're not ready to offer shares of stock, then you may have some difficulty attracting and keeping them. Keep in mind that they are a great talent source because you know their work ethic and capabilities. If you want them to work for you, chances are you have a great deal of trust in them.

If people from your personal network won't join your company, at least reach out to them for hiring recommendations in their network. A referral from someone you trust is a reliable way to find quality talent. Also, reach out to your college alumni association or any professional trade organizations you participated in to find folks who can fill key roles in your organization.

INVEST IN GOOD HR

As soon as you're able to delegate hiring, make your first Human Resources Department hire carefully. These are the people who will not only recruit employees for you but also respond appropriately to any difficulties your employees may encounter.

ALWAYS BE HIRING

Even if you don't have any open positions, keep your eyes and ears out for folks you may want to hire in the future, particularly if you have plans to expand. It's never too early to build a good relationship with a future employee. Whenever you encounter someone promising, keep their résumé handy, and ask them to check in with you every few months to see if any positions have opened.

HIRE SLOW, FIRE FAST

Take your time when it comes to filling key positions at your company. Check out references thoroughly; sometimes even a "positive" reference will reveal vital information about a potential hire if you give them the space to do so. No one is perfect, so be clear-eyed, and make your decisions based on solid, candid information, not just the good stuff that sticks out on a prospect's résumé. By the same token, as unpleasant as it is to fire an employee, postponing the inevitable does neither of you any good. Toxic employees are like cancer cells that can infect other cells. Should you find toxic employees in the mix, move them on quickly and decisively. This is another reason why you need an experienced HR leader and a capable labor attorney who knows your state's labor laws by heart.

SEVENTY-FIVE PERCENT PRODUCTIVITY IS REALLY 100 PERCENT PRODUCTIVITY

Though hard to quantify, the productivity you'll receive from lower-caliber employees is going to be less than what you'll need to make your business run at full speed. Ask any small business owner who's built their business with their own capital. Until you're at a point where you can attract the top-tier workforce you want, you'll have to fill in the remaining

25 percent or so of effort that is still missing. Accepting that situation now will help you balance the frustration you may run into in your hiring efforts.

HANDBOOK

Starting with your employee handbook, policies, and procedures, make sure all your employee paperwork is in order. Then, hire a capable labor attorney and litigator to review your documentation to make doubly sure that it is. You'll need to have a sexual harassment and anti-discrimination policy as well as notices expressing your intolerance for sexual harassment and discrimination in your workplace. Have your labor attorney review your paperwork every two years because labor laws change regularly.

EVALUATIONS

Conduct performance evaluations, and have them accurately documented. Unfortunately, managers will sometimes check any box just to complete the task. I once had a manager arbitrarily give his team high ratings when they were doing average or below average work. Our rating system should be applied consistently. Here's one big reason why: you may someday have a lawsuit to defend, and you will need that performance documentation to have been consistently and fairly applied to justify your actions.

Make sure that your performance evaluations accurately reflect your staff's roles and responsibilities. This way when you articulate your staff's performance, you can objectively provide feedback to the areas where they are meeting your expectations or failing to meet your expectations. To do this, you must have roles and responsibilities written and stored for every role in your company.

EXITING THE BUSINESS

It's immensely fulfilling to be successful in your own business; there's nothing quite like it. In terms of wealth building, though, success must mean more than being able to say, "I created this." Success must include strong profitability. Always remember that what you're building through your business is a wealth-producing engine, not a monument. The profits you earn as a business owner must be reinvested—either back into your business, securities, real estate, and whatever other investment vehicles make up your personal wealth-building plan. I've known too many people who treat their businesses as lifestyle machines, using the profits to buy glittery, depreciating toys until there's no profit left to live on or invest with, not to mention leaving any sort of generational wealth to their heirs. Early on, I was guilty of this same mistake until, thankfully, my Millionaire Mentors provided the guidance I needed to develop a proper exit strategy.

There will eventually come a time when you'll want to move on from your business. Perhaps you'll grow tired of the business' ups and downs, or maybe you'll want to start a new business or follow a different dream like retirement. Believe it or not, the best time to plan your exit strategy may be *before* you get into business, not afterwards. When you analyze the business you're considering owning, it's enormously helpful to already have your possible exit strategy or endgame in mind. If you're going to think long term, the smart way to do so is to think things through to the end whenever possible.

These are five options available to successfully exit a business and move on to the next phase in your life. They are:

- Stacking cash and dissolving the business
- Merging the business

- Selling the business
- Taking the business public
- Building a legacy by passing it on

Each of these strategies helps to ensure that you won't have spent all that blood, sweat, and tears with nothing to show for it in the end. Millionaires know better than to come up empty-handed.

STACKING CASH AND DISSOLVING THE BUSINESS

I like baseball, which is a game of strategy, and that's why I call this first exit plan the "Base Hit" strategy. It gets you to Destination Millionaire and beyond one base hit at a time rather than making you swing for the fences and risk striking out. Here's how it works: every year that you make a profit, no matter how large or small, take all the cash you can out of the business and reinvest it in securities, real estate, and/or alternative investments (more on the latter in the next section). By "all the cash you can," I mean what's left after you pay your taxes and set aside the cash that you need to prime the business for the first two to three months of a new business year, consistent with your accounts receivable. You must leave some margin (say, 10–15 percent) because not everyone will always pay on time. But the rest of the money goes into building your Freedom Fund.

The beautiful thing about this approach is that once you reach your Freedom Fund or endgame goal, you'll still have the option to close, dissolve, sell, merge, go public, or pass your business on to your children. As you've probably guessed, this is the strategy that I took with my business. For the past twenty-odd years, I've been investing my business profits in securities (stocks, bonds, and commodities), real estate, and private equity. I've paid off all personal debt that isn't being paid off by tenants who rent my properties. My business is debt-free too. The income I earn from my real estate investments coupled with the income generated by my Freedom Fund balance (using the 4 percent rule) can cover my lifestyle for the rest of my days. Ideally, I'd like to grow my Freedom Fund large enough to where dividend income can cover my living expenses in retirement. It's a sure way to preserve my Freedom Fund for the next generation (which is one of two components of generational wealth). I'll probably try to sell my business, though there are no guarantees I'll be able to. The truth is, even if I'm unsuccessful at selling it, I'll have long since used its income generating power to set myself up for life.

Here's a friendly baseball reminder about the effectiveness of this strategy: everyone knows that Hank Aaron, the home run king, made it to the Baseball Hall of Fame. But so did a guy named Sam Rice, who built an enduring legacy for the ages simply by stacking base hits.

MERGING THE BUSINESS

Earlier we discussed how a merger involves joining forces with a similar company in your industry. If that becomes your chosen strategy, rather than stacking cash, you should be reinvesting it in your business to constantly increase its valuation prior to any merger. More outlets, more offices, more products, more employees, and higher EBITDA—anything that you know will make your business more valuable should be undertaken.

Merging with another company is a major step that, once you agree to it, there's no turning back. You will likely have to cede some power and control in a merger. There will undoubtedly be some actions taken in the new company that you won't agree with. Therefore, during the due diligence period that precedes a merger, you'll need to fully understand how the company you're merging with conducts its business. Their business culture will have to align closely with yours; otherwise, you could be in trouble. It's as though you're getting married without a prenuptial agreement or a chance to date or live together first. So, get to know the management team and talk to the employees. Ask around about the company from several sources, including their customers or clients, and see if things add up. You'll want to know their corporate policies and procedures, what their work culture is like, and what their reputation is in the marketplace. You can't simply leave it up to your business broker or attorney; they're well-paid matchmakers who don't have to live with your decision for the next decade or more. You do. Find the right company to merge with or choose another exit strategy. Much as in love, timing plays an important role in any merger. The right company, at the wrong time, is not a good match.

SELLING THE BUSINESS

Successfully selling a business is the embodiment of the entrepreneurial dream; like a grand slam home run in the bottom of the ninth inning that wins the World Series. Nonetheless, depending on the circumstances surrounding your eventual sale, you may experience a certain degree of wistfulness or nostalgia about it. It's hard to give up a business that's become a big part of your life, but hopefully, the wealth and satisfaction that come along with successfully selling your business will be more than sufficient to dry any tears you may experience.

To sell your business, you'll need to first know the true value of your business. That's not what it's worth to you, but rather what potential buyers or investors would be willing to pay for it. As mentioned, companies are usually sold at a multiple of EBITDA. A knowledgeable business broker in your industry can help you determine that value. You'll want someone from your industry because they'll have a clear understanding of your business' nuances as well as its intrinsic and extrinsic value. Put another way, they won't allow you to leave money on the table that you might not have identified in the first place. They'll also have a network of other businesses in your industry who are looking to expand, and thus, they can potentially connect you to prospective buyers.

When thinking about your company's sale price, you must be sure to calculate your business broker's "success" fee as well. It might be structured like a step deal, meaning something like 10 percent on the first $1 million of valuation, and a lower percentage on larger increments, up to the full-sale price. You'll have accountant and attorney fees to consider as well. These are all negotiable, provided you negotiate them before the sale, not at the time of the sale.

Business brokers are not cheap. They're typically paid a retainer fee plus a "success" fee. Their retainer covers the preparation of your offer package which includes your business capabilities, financials, company valuation, and listing price. In my industry, for example, the retainer for a highly skilled broker can cost as much as $50,000 upfront. Last time I checked, that's not chump change, but it's money well-spent because choosing the wrong broker can lead to disaster.

Before you hand over your financials and initial broker fee to anyone, be sure you've carefully interviewed them and know how many deals they've executed over the past ten years. Ask them what's the current multiple on EBITDA in today's market for businesses like yours. For example, if your company's annual EBITDA is $100,000, are buyers paying twice that, or something more like five or ten times that amount? In the first instance, you might elect to simply hang on for another two years, make the money yourself, and sell the business at a more opportune time. Ask your broker for at least five references of businesses they've helped to exit in the past couple years and check those references. Your business (not to mention all that money) is your baby; treat it with the care and watchfulness it deserves.

Once you've determined the true value of your business and have considered the options with your business broker, you can evaluate and choose the right exit strategy. Work closely on this with your broker; going solo can easily result in you getting taken advantage of and losing out on a lot of money. If you decide to dissolve your business, your accountant and attorney can help instead.

When your EBITDA reaches and maintains its highest possible level over several years, you're ready, along with your broker, to try to sell the company. Likely buyers may include larger competitors, as well as private equity firms looking to roll your business into another. No matter the buyer, you may not receive an all-cash offer. Businesses are frequently acquired through a combination of cash and stock, either in the company making the purchase or, in the event of a merger, stock in the combined entity being created. If stock is part of the sale, then you must carefully evaluate the price of your would-be purchaser's stock. Is it worth its current value? Is it likely to appreciate or depreciate? How might the acquisition of your business affect that company's stock price?

Even after you've established your business' value, as we said at the beginning of this chapter, things are only worth what someone will pay for them, even if the price seems right or fair. You may get lowballed. If what the buyer is offering you (minus the broker fee and before tax) is an amount that equates to less than three years of the cash you're taking out of the business *and* you're confident you can continue to take that same amount of cash out of the business for the next three to five years, then I suggest you walk away from the deal. That figure will vary by individual and personal needs, though to my mind, you need to receive at least four to five years of pre-tax cash flow to make a sale worth your while.

GOING PUBLIC WITH THE BUSINESS

Are you the next Facebook or Netflix with breakneck user-growth continuing through the foreseeable future? Or the next Tesla—first to market and miles ahead of the competition for your type of product? Then you may want to exit your company by taking it public. In doing so, you allow the public as well as institutional investors to buy shares of your company while you retain control over how the company will operate and/or expand. The typical threshold for companies that wish to go public is $100 million in revenues. But hey, this can still be you someday.

To take your business public, you need to hire lawyers and accountants who are specialized in IPOs (initial public offerings). They and the entire process are extremely expensive. Before you get too deep in the process, they will perform an upfront analysis to assess whether you truly have what it takes to go public. The thing to know is that while your ownership stake goes down, the value of that ownership can go through the roof when you issue an IPO. Multimillionaires and billionaires are often minted overnight, though clearly, that's not always the case. Sometimes a business is overvalued at the time of its IPO, and once the initial excitement of a stock wears off, the reality of the bottom line can set in and drive its share price down.

The steps necessary to go public are far too complex for our context, though there's no reason to exclude an IPO exit from your dreams. The more market share you can capture, and the higher you can drive your EBITDA, the closer you'll bring your business to someday ringing the bell symbolizing the opening of a trading day on the New York Stock Exchange, with your company firmly in the mix.

BUILDING A LEGACY AND PASSING IT ON

You don't have to own a billion-dollar business enterprise to create a legacy business. What matters most is that the business you build can stand the test of time. Ask anyone who thought buying and selling typewriters would make a good legacy business, and you'll see what I mean quickly. The need that the business satisfies in the marketplace must be a lasting need, at least for the next several generations, for a legacy to endure.

Along with meeting that essential criterion, the right values and practices must be instilled in each generation so that they can pass the torch and keep the flame glowing in the family legacy business for generations to come, whether it's a real estate company, or a local restaurant specialized in chili dogs. If your heirs won't have the care and commitment to maintaining profitability in the business, they and the enterprise itself are doomed to fail.

In choosing legacy as an exit strategy, you must be careful not to allow your own hubris to blind you to the desires of others. Do your kids truly want to take over for you someday? Are they willing to dive in now or when they're of an appropriate age to test the waters and see what it's like? Are they suited to the tasks required in running your business? The last thing you want is to create unhappiness in your family, especially at the price of losing a business you've poured your heart and soul into.

Assuming this is the right way to go for you and yours, reinvesting in your business must be done continuously, not only to increase the valuation but to ensure that you're keeping up with the times in terms of items like technology. You may have your way of doing things, but as you ready the business for the transition, you need to prepare for the next generation who doesn't know or care to find out what a word processor does or what a ledger sheet looks like. In short, you must continuously modernize if you hope to entice future generations.

Not only do you have to be open to new ways of working, but you must also be realistic about your family members as well. If they don't already have a passion for your business, your kids may someday develop it over time, though if that's the case, then please heed these words of caution: don't choose legacy as your exit strategy. You wouldn't marry someone hoping they'd someday fall in love with you, I presume, so why take that risk with your business? A good rule of thumb is this: family first, family business second.

HOW TO BECOME A MILLIONAIRE THROUGH ENTREPRENEURSHIP

Step One—Choose the right business using the evaluation criteria provided earlier. To secure initial funding, continue earning more and paying and consuming less until you've reached Level 6 on the M$M investment ladder, or seek out friends, family, an angel investor, or a venture capitalist to fund your business. The exact amount you need will vary by choice of business.

Step Two—Create a comprehensive business plan for your chosen business within the industry type, business model, and legal structure that best matches it.

Step Three—Identify and select a business exit strategy that can get you to your desired endgame.

Step Four—Get your business started, and run it until it becomes a well-oiled machine. Use your exit strategy as a guiding principle, and execute according to your business plan.

Step Five—Take your profits, and reinvest them in the business, or take them out, and invest them in securities, real estate, or alternative investments. Expand your business into new product and service offerings and new markets. Focus on increasing your revenue, optimizing your expenses, and growing your EBITDA.

Step Six (optional)—If legacy is your "why," teach the inner workings of your business to your heirs, and put them in the driver's seat (while you sit in the front passenger seat) until you're ready to fully pass the business along to the next generation.

Step Seven—Once you achieve your long-term business goals, dissolve the business, sell it, merge it with another business, take it public, or pass it on to your heirs.

SUPPLEMENTAL
CHAPTER 4

INVESTING IN ALTERNATIVE INVESTMENTS

IF YOU'RE READING THIS SECTION BECAUSE YOU'VE REACHED Level 7 on my M$M investment ladder, then let me pause to congratulate you. You've achieved Destination Millionaire, and now, thinking like a millionaire, you're looking to see where else you can grow your wealth for the future. Nice work, *playa*. If you're not at Level 7 yet, I still want you to keep reading because you may find yourself looking for alternative investments for your business, and if there's one thing we've learned on this journey, it's that it pays to know what makes the other guy tick, be they your competitor or a potential investor in your business. So, stick around as we dive into this ever-evolving category of alternative investment (AI) opportunities, which include angel investing, venture capital, hedge funds, and private equity.

Whereas investing in stocks and bonds might net an average profit in the range of 5–10 percent per year, what you're trying to accomplish as an AI investor is 25–50 percent annual returns and up. For example, let's say someone was starting another Black-owned movie studio like Tyler Perry's, and you wanted to invest. A new movie studio is a tall order for anyone to accomplish, given that most movies end up losing money instead of making it. On the other hand, Tyler Perry found a way through his immense talent and perseverance to create a small empire, so maybe someone else can do it too. Movie investing is extremely high risk, but its upside potential is gigantic, with some movies grossing as much as $1 billion at the box office.

How about a startup seeking several million dollars to develop motors that run on hydrogen? Or a new translation service that relies exclusively on robots? Believe it or not, these highly speculative investments are exactly the types that fall within the category of alternative investments. High-risk leading to high reward or, to borrow from our previous analogy, potential triples and home runs, in place of base hits. That's a key reason that millionaires in alternative investments have highly paid, clever accountants who know how to turn their investment losses into tax write-offs. It allows them to be far less daunted in the face of big risks.

By the way, the term "millionaire" in this instance isn't simply a loosey-goosey description of your wealth. It's a precise dollars-and-cents thing. To participate in alternative investing, you must be what's called an accredited investor, which means you'll need to satisfy at least one of the following criteria:

- Have a net worth more than $1 million.
- Demonstrate annual income more than $200,000 (or $300,000 if you file jointly) for at least the past two years, with an expectation to continue that level of earning at minimum for the

following year. No mixing is allowed, meaning you can't show $300,000 jointly one year and then only $200,000 for one individual the next.

- Be a general partner, director, or executive officer of the company that is issuing the unregulated security.
- Demonstrate previous job experience or a sufficient level of education that demonstrates professional knowledge of the unregulated securities that make up alternative investing.

The purpose of these SEC requirements is to provide protection to investors and ensure they can withstand a total loss in these risky investments without getting wiped out. That's life in the Big Time, where money talks, and...well, I'll let you fill in the rest.

ANGEL INVESTING

Angel investing is much like how it sounds; a wealthy investor or "angel" waves the equivalent of their magic wallet at an investment opportunity, such as an early-stage startup business, and that investment helps the business develop, market, and sell their product, service, and business model. Angels are unincorporated individuals, which, as we'll see, is in large part what differentiates them from venture capitalists. However, with all types of alternative investing, there's a lot of overlap. Angels typically fund businesses in the earliest stages of development. Daymond John, founder of FUBU, is probably one of the better known angel investors in the African American community, though there are countless others, including his counterparts on the show *Shark Tank* and—for the past five years—yours truly. Recently, more and more angel investors have been banding together as groups based on their affinities, such as wanting to invest in Black-owned businesses. This is a potential boon to businesses looking to find angel investors because they can be more easily targeted based on their interests and vice versa. Not to mention the cumulative financial power of a group of angel investors versus that of one single angel investor.

For our purposes, let's focus on what to look for in an investment opportunity as an angel investor, what risks you will run, as well as ways to mitigate those risks. In the section on Entrepreneurship, we talked about the need for entrepreneurs to put together a comprehensive and compelling business plan. For an angel, that is the first place to start when trying to decide whether an investment in a particular business makes sense for you. Is there a written business plan, and is it coherent, compelling, and comprehensive? Does the founder have a track record for successfully creating and exiting businesses? Is a strong management team already in place, or will there be one put into place in short order? Does the business idea make logical sense? It can even be a so-called "moonshot" idea, such as Elon Musk or Richard Branson's recent explorations into space travel and Hyper Loops; what must matter to you is whether the steps outlined in the business plan follow a logical plan towards eventual profitability. Imagine that the moonshot idea eventually comes to fruition. Is there then a solid structure in place to ensure when and how you'll receive your well-earned profits? You don't want to invest in something without a timely plan to pay back your investment as well as the profits you hope to realize.

Angel investment capital requirements come in all shapes and sizes, though they tend to start at around $50,000, with a sweet spot for most high-net-worth investors of about $250,000 per investment. More sophisticated deals may require capital in the millions. Angel investment opportunities typically arise through word of mouth or referral, though there are also online resources such as Crunchbase that can connect you to companies looking for angel funding.

An opportunity to invest might look like this: Let's say one of your investor friends introduces you to someone who has a great idea for how to build a better electric battery for cars. At first, they're going to need to do a lot of research and development (R&D) to develop a prototype, and then, assuming the battery works the way they need it to, they'll need to figure out how to mass produce and distribute it. An inventor or company at this stage is a good example of where you might want to invest as an angel investor; someone with an interesting and potentially industry-changing idea who's still in the early stages of development. Likely they'll be seeking a specific amount of capital in return for a set percentage of equity ownership in their company. That's called their "ask." Before you respond to that ask with your offer, you as an investor need to first determine if their valuation of the company makes sense. For example, 10 percent equity in exchange for $50,000 gives a valuation of $500,000. At this stage, they may not have any sales, which means that all predictions of future revenues are speculative at best. What's the potential upside of the deal? That's something you can "game out" by looking at whatever future sales projections they've put together in their business plan and using your understanding of the business and industry. You should always verify a startup's valuation with industry experts and accountants. With no track record or historical revenue to glean from the company's past, all valuation is purely speculative at best. As with any investment, you need to measure the risk versus the potential reward, but the business valuation estimated by the owner is a good indicator of how well a business owner understands their business. If it seems reasonable, that's a good sign; too high or too low could be an indicator of potential trouble ahead.

Whenever you consider an angel investment deal, be sure to consult beforehand with an attorney, an industry expert, and an accountant because, even if your investment is successful, your angel investments may be subject to a different taxation category. As of this writing, the US tax code favors investors in certain riskier investment classes by giving their capital gains a different name, "carried interest," and by taxing those gains at a far lower rate. That's a circumstance that may change over time, so be sure you and your accountant review the latest rules governing alternative investments.

VENTURE CAPITAL INVESTING

Venture capital firms or individuals, or VCs as they are commonly known, are a step up from angel investors. Whereas angel investors fund companies as they develop and begin to implement their ideas, products, and services, VCs generally help scale a company that's already further along with its business model, has long-term potential, and needs capital to grow exponentially. Uber is an example of a VC-funded company, as was Facebook in its early days; companies that can quickly grow large are prime targets for infusions of venture capital. Although VC is a form of private equity, what differentiates it from private equity firms is that VCs invest in emerging companies, not well-established ones.

Because VCs are pitched business ideas about as often as pancakes are flipped at IHOP, they're extremely scrupulous about which companies they decide to invest in. Venture capital funding happens in rounds, and each round has its own valuation based on performance to that point. The later a VC is to invest, the less equity they'll typically receive for their investment because the valuation will be higher than in previous rounds. If it's not, that may be a bad sign for the company, or at least for you as a potential investor. The endgame for a VC is usually an initial public offering (IPO), also known as taking a company public (allowing others to buy its stock), acquisition by another company at a higher valuation than at the time of the VC investment, or a merger with another company. The time horizon for each of these varies a great deal though they tend to occur at around five years, plus or minus a year or so.

For an individual investor like you who may not be ultra-wealthy ($100 million plus net worth and $10 million plus in cash), there are venture capital funds that allow you to be part of a VC "play" without the responsibility of hearing the pitches and selecting the companies to take a risk on. As such, your responsibility is limited to doing your due diligence about any VC fund you invest in (more on the due diligence process shortly). Make no mistake: it's a big responsibility. You need to find out what the VC's track record is thus far. What types of businesses have they helped scale? Have they taken any of the businesses they've funded public? How well are those businesses doing in the stock market? Which businesses that they've funded have ended up as disappointments or failures? What's the experience of their management team?

Perhaps you have a particular interest in helping Black-owned businesses (BOBs), and I hope you will; if so, has the VC fund you're exploring worked with any successful BOBs, and if so, how have they done? The more and deeper questions you ask, the better the likelihood of you finding the right place to make your investment.

HEDGE FUND INVESTING

Hedge funds are made up of pools of high-net-worth investors, including the hedge fund manager responsible for the funds' investment decisions. They are known for the innovative investment strategies they use, as well as the often out-sized returns they're able to generate through those investments. Despite their name, hedge funds don't always "hedge" or counterbalance their investments as much as one might think. They use massive amounts of leverage, meaning borrowed money. Back in 1994, a so-called "short" position taken by a single hedge fund known as Long-Term Capital Management not only bankrupted the fund but also nearly destroyed the entire Western economy. In the high-risk world of hedge funds, too much leverage at the wrong time can lead to disaster.

Hedge funds frequently purchase controlling shares in large, well-known public corporations and attempt to turn around their business models. They are also permitted by Securities and Exchange Commission (SEC) rules to take short positions in a company, which means they can bet with their investments not only that a company will succeed (known as being "long"), but they can also go short if they think a company will do poorly and make enormous profits if their prediction—long or short—turns out to be correct.

Many hedge fund managers come from the world of mutual funds, but be careful not to confuse the two; hedge funds are enormously riskier. Hedge funds adopt many different investment strategies and sometimes play the role of market detectives. They look for inefficiencies in the market and try to capitalize on them. Hedge funds are free to invest in whatever they choose.

Consequently, there are many types of hedge funds and many strategies they employ to make money. An equity hedge fund might seek out under or overvalued stocks, bonds, or even stock indexes like the NASDAQ or, internationally, the NIKKEI index in Japan. A macro hedge fund might look for global interest rates that don't jibe with a country's economic policies. A hedge fund focused on volatility might seek to exploit how others are invested in particular stocks by looking for possible imbalances between long and short positions. A currency-focused hedge fund might seek to profit from inefficiencies like an undervalued peso or an overvalued Euro.

One key differentiator of hedge funds for you as an investor is their compensation model, which is structured according to what's called the two and twenty model. Investors receive a percentage of the profits based on the size of your investment. The hedge fund manager who makes the buying and selling decisions for the investors receives 20 percent of any profits the fund makes each year, as well as a 2 percent annual management fee, no matter how well or poorly the fund performs. While that may seem like a lot of profits and fees to give to one person, a key reason wealthy investors flock to hedge funds, beyond the enormous returns they can generate, is that hedge fund managers always have a sizeable amount of skin in the game as well. That 20 percent of the profits is a powerful incentive for them to make money. That makes them far more likely to do whatever it takes not to lose anyone's money. Hedge fund managers also tend to be some of the brightest minds in finance. Excessive pride or self-confidence, rather than a lack of intelligence, is what often trips them up.

HOW TO INVEST IN HEDGE FUNDS

A minimum investment in a hedge fund starts at around $100,000 and can range up into the millions. As mentioned, that money gets locked up for a certain period, so be sure you find out how long the lockup period is and that you won't need access to your capital anytime before it ends. You'll have to do some research to see which funds are currently accepting new investors, using online resources such as E-vestment, though a financial adviser or one of your mentors may be your best bet. You may care what a hedge fund invests in, or you may simply be focused on performance in terms of return on investment. In the latter case, remember that hedge fund managers often move from fund to fund in their careers, so their past performance may extend beyond the hedge fund you presently have in your crosshairs. My advice is to investigate them thoroughly because both the successful and the unsuccessful move around quite a bit.

PRIVATE EQUITY INVESTING

Private equity (PE) also draws from pools of high-net-worth investors, including Level 7 investors such as you. PE looks to purchase a controlling interest in private companies or properties and take over their management to generate profit, or they may seek to purchase a publicly traded company and take it private. In PE, return on investment is the name of the game. It's worth mentioning that the differences between PE and, say, hedge funds are not etched in stone. Hedge funds sometimes perform investment activities that overlap with those of PE funds. However, venture capital firms more closely resemble private equity funds, a key difference being that PE works with well-established companies rather than startups or up-and-comers as VCs do.

Private equity firms often provide higher returns than what can be obtained by investing in publicly traded companies. The starting point for investing in a PE firm is usually around $250,000, a bar that is generally too high for most folks. However, the average investor can invest in PE by purchasing the publicly traded stock of a PE fund managed by a firm, such as the Blackstone Group or Apollo Global Management. There are also highly diversified exchange-traded funds (ETFs) made up of private equity firms which can be bought by any investor.

One good example of a private equity deal is a real estate syndicate. A syndicate pools funds from passive investors to make a real estate investment in multi-family or commercial real estate and provide a specific return to its investors. The syndicator will identify a property for investment, do the work of raising the money for the investment, manage the day-to-day operations, and may invest anywhere from 0–20 percent of their own money in an LLC set up specifically for the purpose of the purchase. Investors then provide the remaining 80–100 percent of the total capital required to acquire and sometimes make property upgrades. Investors earn money the same way they do in other real estate investments: namely, through rental income, rental increases, and property appreciation. The syndicator has a fiduciary responsibility to define the risks and returns of the investment and to protect it.

Profits are distributed according to how long it takes for the syndicate's investment to begin making a profit; that can be as little as four months to a year or as much as several years from the time of initial investment. The syndicate frequently receives an acquisition fee upfront, which is their reward for having put the deal together. The good news for you as an investor is that once that fee is paid, you are next in line for profit sharing. The preferred return you'll receive tends to range between 5–10 percent annually, after which the syndicate can share in the profits as well. Preferred returns are paid out monthly, quarterly, or annually depending on the guidelines of the syndicate's operating agreement. This type of structure helps incentivize syndicates to prioritize return on investment for their investors, such as you.

HOW TO INVEST IN PRIVATE EQUITY

While real estate syndication and other PE deals typically come via word of mouth or referral, nowadays there are crowdfunding alternatives for investors who aren't otherwise connected, such as Crowdstreet or Fundrise. These platforms analyze deal opportunities and then present them to accredited investors, along with a plethora of information about each project online. What's nice too is that they don't necessarily require investment as sizable as deals you may hear about through your own existing network; the entry threshold is lower and more accessible.

To draw on an example from one of my own PE investments, five years ago, I bought into a syndication group in Florida that invests in large three-hundred- to four-hundred-door multi-family properties in Colorado, Texas, Florida, and a few other states. The group has over four hundred investors in their network, enabling it to raise capital within forty-eight hours to acquire properties selling for as much as $40–60 million. The minimum investment size is $100,000 per deal, which represents one equity unit. I'm typically given twenty-four to forty-eight hours to confirm my commitment to a deal and about thirty days to submit my capital. The syndicate offers a preferred return of 7–10 percent annually, and the investors share in 70 percent of the profit after the properties are sold, with the syndicator receiving the remaining 30 percent of the profit. The preferred returns are paid monthly, and monthly payments are issued four months after the close date. The syndication group manages the property and takes care of updating the amenities of the property and the apartment units. They raise rents annually by 3 percent, thereby increasing the net income of the property over time. Five to seven years later, the property is sold at a higher value because, by then, it's been nicely upgraded and yielding high-net income. When all is said and done, investors typically receive an overall 14–17 percent annualized return on average, including their preferred return, over the five-to-seven-year holding period.

Overall, this type of investment has worked out well for me. There are always some risks which can impact ROI; of late, job losses due to COVID-19 damaged our ability to attract new tenants, which in turn impacted our net income. As a result, the syndication manager is not distributing preferred returns on certain properties. My diversification strategy for syndicate investments is to invest in multiple property deals in different markets and regions. This way, if my Texas deals start struggling, my deals in Colorado, Florida, and Georgia can act as hedges until Texas recovers. I particularly like that my investments are tied to a tangible asset, rather than a business whose value can quickly fluctuate for the worse. The not-so-good news is that, unlike properties that I personally own and manage, I have no control over how things are managed because I am just one of probably one hundred or more investors in each property. Nonetheless, as a wealth-growing strategy, real estate syndicates certainly deserve a closer look.

Following are some of the pros and cons to investing in alternative investments. As you can see, the risks and the rewards represent opposites, with no one between them to assist you, except, perhaps, your mentors.

PROS	CONS
You can grow your capital quickly and significantly, without any direct effort.	It's extremely risky, including the possibility of losing your entire investment.
It's a fascinating investment class that exposes you to many different industries up close.	It is prone to fraud by unethical operators and hucksters.
It's a major and proven source of wealth building among the wealthy.	You have little to no control of what happens to your money once you invest it.
Networking with other high-net-worth individuals can open you up to other investment opportunities.	It's unregulated and not guaranteed by the FDIC.
You don't have the hassle of dealing with tenant calls and complaints, nor maintenance and repair issues.	Investment sizes are large which increases the risk of significant losses.

I've only been an investor in alternative investing deals for five years. The experience has been eye-opening, to say the least. Some deals have worked out well for me while others have not. As a person who typically manages their own investments, I've felt extremely vulnerable at times because, although investors like me are given detailed reports on a regular basis, we still can't touch the investment or "kick the tires" of whatever we're investing in. We're entirely at the mercy of the fund manager. Nevertheless, investing in alternative investments has worked out well for me.

RISKS ASSOCIATED WITH INVESTING IN ALTERNATIVE INVESTMENTS

There are several risks associated with all forms of alternative investments. Here are some of the risks to be aware of before investing in the AI category.

ANGEL INVESTING

As an angel investor, it's easy to fall in love with ideas and miss red flags, such as a poorly assessed valuation. By the same token, it's easy to fall in love with the owner and managers and miss red flags when it comes to the idea. Beware of both tendencies. Great salespeople don't always make great managers, just as mediocre ideas don't necessarily flourish under great management. As an angel investor, your decision criteria should include an idea you strongly believe in, a sound and reasonable business plan, a clear pathway to profitability, and a person or management team you feel could succeed at anything. There are so many investment opportunities out there; if you're going to take a big risk, be sure you fully believe in the people and ideas you take on. If not, move on to the next business pitch. You'll find the right fit eventually.

Startups, like all companies, raise capital at different times and at different valuations. The risk you run as an angel investor is that your investment can become diluted over time or wiped out if the business fails. The earlier you get in, the more equity you can usually demand for your investment, but that's not always the case. As the company continues raising money, which startups tend to do, your investment can become progressively less valuable. Another common risk in angel investing, for several reasons, is a company overpromising or under-delivering in terms of product and/or timing. Maybe that hydrogen-source idea pans out, but what if it takes ten years longer than anticipated to get there? What if a competitor has come up with the same solution in only four years or for half the price of what your startup can deliver? What if the company needs another million dollars to get over the hump and can't find new investors? The list is endless. A startup, by its very definition, is a company that is only beginning. It does not have a long track record (although the owner and management team hopefully do with other companies). Hence, the high degree of risk.

VENTURE CAPITAL INVESTING

The risks associated with being a VC investor or participating in a VC fund are like those of being an angel investor. The difference is that with a VC, you're investing at one level further removed; you're essentially using the VC as your investment proxy. This type of investing might not be right if you consider yourself more of a hands-on type of investor.

HEDGE FUNDS

As an individual investor in a hedge fund, you must trust that the hedge fund manager has the business acumen backed by impeccable research to make the right choices with your money. Since your money is temporarily locked up, you have no recourse should things take a turn for the worse.

Given the size of your investment, the stakes are high, and the losses can be significant if not total. As an accredited investor, simply because you can theoretically afford to lose your shirt doesn't mean you should run the risk of it. One incorrect "short" or too much leverage can often be all it takes.

PRIVATE EQUITY INVESTING

PE firms bet huge sums of money, including yours, that a particular company or companies will eventually capture a larger market share and/or grow profits significantly. Without a crystal ball and given the whims of the marketplace, those bets can be wrong, leading to major losses for investors.

Fortunately, PE investment strategies can involve loaning money (debt financing) to companies in exchange for equity and interest. That means you may have to wait a long time to profit from your investment. If the deal includes a guaranteed return, as many real estate syndications do, you'll receive interest on your investment for as long as the investment is profitable, thereby mitigating your overall risk. However, if you run into periods of time when the investment is not making a profit, your guaranteed return can be frozen indefinitely. Therefore, ask the tough questions, so you know the inherent risks, and be sure you can stomach them before getting involved.

PERFORMING DUE DILIGENCE ON ALTERNATIVE INVESTMENT DEALS

If, like me, you're somewhat reluctant to invest in anything at arm's length, I can offer you these tips to follow before you offer up a bag of your hard-earned money for someone else to grow for you. We millionaires need to keep growing our money with confidence, not a hope and a prayer that someone else can grow it because they're a good salesperson.

ALWAYS CHECK REFERENCES

This is a universal management rule for all your investments, and it too often falls by the wayside. If possible, you want personal references from someone you know well, who values their money as much or more than you. If you don't know anyone who fits that bill, ask the fund manager for a list of previous and current investors, and reach out to them for references. Naturally, any references a fund manager gives you will be someone who will speak well of them, but if you listen patiently and ask probing questions, they may reveal some useful details they might not have otherwise. Get three to five references, and call those people to see what their experience has been. Of those, ask for a couple deals or situations where they didn't make money or even lost it. Find out how the fund manager handled the situation. Were they transparent about the situation? Did they keep investors informed, or did they run, hide, or become difficult to communicate with? Put in the work, and be adamant about getting solid references. Let the fund managers know that you can't go forward if they won't put you in contact with at least one or two investors who lost money on a deal with them. Here's why: everyone runs into challenging times in business. It comes with the territory. What matters is how you treat investors during those tough times, not how you throw parties for them in good times. If a manager says they've never experienced hard times, run! You don't want to be the guinea pig. You've worked diligently for your money and don't have to find out the hard way whether the group you're investing with is honorable or not. Trust is built through moments of adversity, not moments of calm. Trust, or a lack thereof, must always be a primary factor in your investment decision.

DON'T BE AFRAID TO RATTLE THE CAGE

Once you give your hard-earned cash away, it can get difficult to check up on your investments. These days most funds have online apps for investors to check on their investments and returns, but sometimes you need to talk with people to get a true sense of how things are going. Investment managers can be ruthless and unscrupulous, and the bad ones will scam you if you're not careful. Generally, arrogant investors are the easiest to scam because they don't do their homework. My advice is to check up on things and periodically rattle the cage. For instance, if you're investing in a piece of real estate, drive by the property, and look around. Make sure it's real. Check the property records to be sure that the LLC you joined owns the property. Never invest in real estate if your name is not listed in the LLC that owns the property. Stop by the property management office. Ask them how things are going; are tenants paying on time, or are things problematic? No matter what type of investment you've made, this level of scrutiny is your best and only chance to be sure you don't end up victimized like Bernie Madoff's investors did (and countless others). Many of the smartest people in America lost millions of dollars in Madoff's Ponzi scheme because nobody was checking up on what he was doing. It's nice to be smart, but diligence—not intelligence—is the secret sauce to successful alternative investing.

KEEP IT REAL AND KEEP IT SMALL

I rarely invest in new private businesses that don't have any assets. I don't invest in dreams; I prefer tangible assets like buildings or businesses with intellectual property, inventory, or products that have value. On the rare occasion when I do invest in a new private business, I limit my investment to a small sum, especially at first. I do this because as a business owner myself, I know what it takes to run a business successfully, and part of it is luck. There are too many moving parts in a business to predict its success without some form of testing in the marketplace itself. If you're going to take a chance on an investment, that's up to you. Just be sure to do so with money you won't be devastated to lose.

It may be worth hiring an experienced accountant, industry consultant, and attorney who understand startup businesses, hedge funds, and private equity to look over any deals you're seriously considering. They will know what kind of due diligence is necessary to ensure that your investment is safe. If they can't vouch for the deal, then you must be willing to walk away and possibly lose out on the next Amazon startup. Don't worry, there will be many other opportunities to come. It pays to have a trusted team of money professionals that you believe in and, most importantly, listen to. And even if you decide not to take their advice, be sure your accountant and attorney review any agreements *before* you sign them. If you can't afford an attorney or accountant, that may be a sign that you can't afford to invest in alternative investments either. Keep grinding until you've got your capital up sufficiently, and then hire a professional to help watch your back.

DON'T BELIEVE THE HYPE; VERIFY IT

There are legions of folks out there who throw their money around carelessly. This is yet another reason why it's so important to have millionaire mentors and surround yourself with people who truly value their money, as opposed to worshipping it. As part of your due diligence, find out if there are any pending lawsuits against the fund or fund managers you're considering investing with. The existence of lawsuits doesn't necessarily mean something is wrong—litigation is commonplace at this level of investing—but you need to do some digging to be sure.

NO SIGNATURE MEANS NO MONEY

Never hand over any money for an investment until all the documents are reviewed by a qualified investment attorney and are signed and countersigned. That may seem obvious, but you'd be surprised at how many people, after finally deciding to go all in, hand over their money before receiving a countersigned deal agreement. Most PE managers won't provide you wiring instructions until everything is countersigned, though time and again investors wire money pending a few minor changes in the contract. Unfortunately, once you send money, your negotiating power goes away right along with it. If you're feeling rushed to send money before the contracts have been fully signed and executed, take that as a sign that something may not be entirely right about this deal, at least for you. Otherwise, review and finalize the agreements before you sign. Then, once you receive the countersigned document, go ahead and send the investment funds.

MAKE SURE THERE'S AN ENTREPRENEUR ON THE TEAM

I always ask myself this question when making an investment in a business via an angel, VC, or private equity investment in which I'm to be a "silent" partner: who's going to dive for the loose balls and keep the business in the game? Who's going to be the hero who will save the company from failure? Who's going to take up the slack and keep the business moving when any key personnel quit? If you're investing in a business as an angel investor or VC investor, you need to make sure that there's an entrepreneur on the team.

Ask who the person is that will know what to do and take on the responsibility if the business you're investing in gets in trouble. Ideally, it'll be the CEO or the CFO. Maybe it's the brilliant sales guy. Whichever the case, you want someone on the team who's going to do everything humanly possible to make sure the business succeeds. The difference between a business owner (even a former business owner) and everyone else is that they not only have a more comprehensive view of things, but they've also accepted the burden of being in charge and are not afraid of it. Their career history is likely to be less about scoring points with the boss and more about scoring profits for the business and its investors.

If I don't get a sense that there is a real entrepreneur on a team, I simply walk away from the deal. It's worked for me before, and I know it'll work for me again. I'll never forget the time I was about to invest $1.2 million in cash in a mortgage company when a key underwriter got cold feet and decided to stay with her existing company. It took our team six months to identify a replacement for her. That troubled me. I could practically see the revenue and profit stagnating, as expenses piled up, thanks to the management team's inability to hire and retain key personnel. I had asked the team who was going to make sure we didn't fail, and no one stepped up. So, I stepped back. It was one of the best decisions I ever made because a mortgage business depends upon talented, reliable people, and if the team couldn't keep the business stacked with them, then we'd have no chance of succeeding. My investment would've gone down the tubes.

NEVER SWIM ALONE

Make sure other accredited investors are part of any deal you buy into. If you find yourself alone, you're almost certainly taking on too much risk. Additional accredited investors are a sign that other potentially smart investors believe in the deal or business as well. This is not a fail-safe solution. In the end, you must do your own research and develop your own rationale as to whether to invest or not. Being the only investor may also be a sign that the investment manager doesn't have enough high-net-worth relationships to keep funds flowing into the business in the event of a cash flow shortage. Your investment will be in jeopardy if the business is unable to continue to raise needed funds. So, never swim alone.

NEVER PUT ALL OF YOUR EGGS IN ONE BASKET

Up to this point, we've discussed diversification as the best risk mitigation strategy no matter the investment. Alternative investing is no different. The more you can spread your investments around, the better your chances of having one or more of them succeed. You're better off with a smaller stake in several investment types than one big stake in a make-or-break investment, especially when 80 percent of new businesses fail to even make it past their first year.[5] Diversification should entail multiple deals across multiple industries and managers. In short, go small, and go wide. It's too dangerous to put all your eggs in one basket, particularly when startup eggs are known for how easily they break.

Now that you know what AI investing is, start small, proceed cautiously as you learn the ropes, and always seek the advice of your millionaire mentors, accountant, industry consultants, and attorney before investing in AI. If in doubt, remember to always follow Warren Buffett's classic rules of investing:

- Rule #1: Never Lose Money
- Rule #2: Never Forget Rule #1

HOW TO BECOME A MILLIONAIRE INVESTING IN ALTERNATIVE INVESTMENTS

Now that you've achieved Destination Millionaire, it's time to put Destination Ultra-Rich or Billionaire in your wealth GPS. If you get there

---

5 "Table 7. Survival of Private Sector Establishments by Opening Year," US Bureau of Labor Statistics, accessed June 15, 2022, https://www.bls.gov/bdm/us_age_naics_00_table7.txt.

before I do, I hope you'll be so kind as to show me the way; otherwise, I promise I'll do you that favor when I arrive. In the meantime, let's continue developing our Millionaire Mindsets, adopting millionaire values, and making Millionaire Money Moves.

www.ingramcontent.com/pod-product-compliance
Lightning Source LLC
Chambersburg PA
CBHW031403180326
41458CB00043B/6591/J